Activate Your Purpose

LESSONS ON WALKING INTO GOD'S PURPOSE FOR YOUR LIFE!

Collin Edwards

Foreword by Jamar Jenkins

Collin Edwards

Cover Design by: Taya Lee

First Printing, 2021

To my grandfather, Lannie Spencer Edwards, I hope this book is "worth a nickel" ...

Contents

Foreword

I have had the distinct pleasure of watching Collin begin walking the journey of this book. I have firmly enjoyed the process of challenging him to push past what is culturally acceptable and digging deeper into the mystery of God-given purpose. The challenges this book presents are ones faced not just by a generation but a culture that wants a "crockpot God," to microwave a blessing. This book will not allow you to stand in "Hot Pocket Faith" anymore. In the book of James 1:4, we are admonished to "let patience have her perfect work, that ye may be perfect and entire, wanting nothing." (KJV) This journey to purpose, when done right will challenge you to learn how to wait on God with full understanding that while you are learning how to wait on God, He is surely preparing destiny for you. Collin is an amazing and very insightful young leader in this world and my sincere prayer is that as he invites you into his journey so that you can find yourself and the element of God that produces legacy.

Humbly Submitted,

Pastor Jamar Jenkins

Introduction

Whenever God calls Abraham to go forward to the land of Canaan, his purpose was already outlined. God says to Abraham, "I will make you into a great nation, and I will bless you;" (Gen. 12:2). Abraham, at that point named Abram (which is significant), receives this grand vision but is subsequently met with tough tasks and responsibilities that immediately test his faith. I believe that the same tests Abraham has to face are also prevalent in our lives today. God has called you to do something spectacular! This can be through your marriage, your career, or even with ministry. God has a special calling for everyone, but it is our responsibility to position ourselves to receive everything that He has for us.

There are many times God gives us glimpses of our purpose, an idea of our calling, or a snapshot of our future. We all have an idea of the thing that we are passionate about. Daily, we all have thoughts about our dream job, car, and even spouse. These are all great things to dream about. However, what if God has given us more to think about. What about your purpose in life? Do you ever say, *"God what am I here for?"* Are you currently stuck trying to figure this out? Trust me! You are not alone. The struggle of finding purpose is very common. Maybe, you think that you have already found your purpose in life! Great! However, if you find yourself trying to understand your "why," then this book is for you! What happens when obstacles in life hold us back from our desires? Are you still willing to trust God in these moments? What if I told you that the obstacles are actually necessary for purpose? Many times in life, when adversity strikes, we stay in the same place waiting for change to happen. However, God is actually waiting for us to get in the right position to receive all that He has for us.

Whenever I began to write this book, I felt exactly like Abraham. I wanted answers to all the questions I had about my life. *Why do I feel frustrated? Why aren't things going the way that I expected?* Have you felt this way before? Okay good, so I am not the only one! What I have come to learn is that there are times that God wants you to trust Him with your questions, and then He will begin to reveal His answer.

Activate Your Purpose is designed to help you through these "questionable" moments in life. This book is designed to help you understand that the roadblocks that you have faced are meant to help you find your purpose. Understand, this is not an ordinary, feel-good, self-help read. This is intended to help you build your relationship with God. Through Him, you will begin to understand what He wants from you. The principles and lessons that are discussed in this book have been developed through my own relationship with Christ. The chapters require you to see Biblical stories from different angles. Each chapter is intended to challenge your thinking. The insight that you'll receive from this book will not only allow you to understand your purpose, but also receive healing in every way, shape, and form.

1

Activate Your Purpose

To understand what it means to "activate your purpose," we must clearly define the word purpose. Purpose is the reason that something exists. There is purpose in everything. You get up and go to work on purpose. You eat every day on purpose. There is daily purpose, such as working out. Then there's longer-term purpose like investing in stocks so that you can retire early. Long story short...everything has purpose. Your life itself has purpose! It is all created to help you with whatever God has called for you to do in this world. Even down to the microscopic level, there is a designed purpose in your biological makeup. There are different types of cells in your body that serve a different purpose. For example, bone cells aren't meant to do the same thing as neurons in your brain. God has created everything about you to serve Him in some way, shape, or form. However, problems in life occur whenever you do not acknowledge the purpose in your own life. You begin to believe that life is meaningless, and you start feeling like you are merely existing instead of living. The confusion about your purpose leads to feelings of worthlessness and introduces you to a masterful supervillain...depression. This mindset of worthlessness is contrary to the way God intends for you to live! God has a unique purpose designed for you, and it is time for you to start realizing it! How are you currently feeling? Frustrated? Lost? Confused? Much like Joseph, maybe you feel like you're in a pit (Genesis 37). Know that God has you in that place for a reason! Don't be discouraged. Just like God brought him out of that place, He has plans to bring you out of your pit and into a life of prosperity! You've got to know that supernatural conversations about you were happening before you were even created. Jeremiah 29:11 says, "For I know the plans I have for you, says the Lord, plans to prosper and not to harm you, plans to give you hope and a future." God's plan is already set in place for you! The question becomes since our purpose is already out there, how do I find it? The exciting thing about purpose is that it resides inside of us. The Bible says, "The purposes of a person's heart are deep waters, but one who has insight draws them out" (Proverbs 20:5). Everything that God creates has purpose, and it is stored right inside of you.

Now your question probably is, *"How do I understand my purpose when it is inside of me?"* The answer is easy, God will help draw it out! As Christians, it is our responsibility to seek God, and He will reveal the purpose that lies within us. Many people are running around each day, chasing potential, and are oblivious to God's purpose for them. I would argue that the problem with today's generation is that many people have yet to activate their purpose. Therefore, a lot of people are living with deactivated purposes. Let's look at a more contemporary example to show you what I mean.

Millions of people around the world have smartphones. A smartphone is a physical device with applications that can be installed with the device's software (for anyone that may need clarification). The added software on your smart device increases productivity and can store tons of information. However, when you think about downloading an app on your smartphone, there are certain occasions where the app makes you go through an extensive sign-up process. Once you have given your name, age, and other information, the next step is usually an activation code. Some apps require you to go to an external source and wait to receive a corresponding text message or call with the code. There are times when the steps associated with creating your profile become cumbersome. After a while, you say to yourself, *"I'll come back and finish it later."*

The same thing happens in our minds daily. We often download stuff in our minds and wait for it to come to fruition. Every year we see this with "New Year's resolutions." Even though resolutions sound cool in January, nothing happens because we have yet to follow the steps for it to be activated. How many of these statements resonate with you: *"I am going to learn a new language," "I will be a better student,"* or *"I will exercise more!"* By the time March rolls around, you become pessimistic because you fail to achieve any of these goals. Downloading is the easy step; however, it's the activation that requires time and patience.

Life's difficulty is not merely speaking things into existence; the hard part happens when it is time to go and get the things that you have spoken. James 2:26 states, "For as the body without the spirit is dead, so faith without works is dead also." Showing that our inner faith must be complemented with our outer works. In the book of Judges, God sends an angel to speak to a young man named Gideon. The angel of the Lord appears under an oak tree. Meanwhile, Gideon is inside threshing wheat in a winepress in order to hide from the opposing Midianites. Now, why doesn't God send the angel to the exact place where Gideon is threshing wheat? God's placement of the angel is designed to show Gideon that he has nothing to fear! Think about it! God comes and sits in the same place that Gideon is afraid to go. The area that seems most terrifying in your life is exactly where God is seated. He is waiting there to give you instructions about your coming breakthrough. God provides your blessings in the place that He expects you to be. Walking in purpose is not easy, but God will never put you through an obstacle that He doesn't have the power to bring you through.

Ask yourself, am I in the right position to receive what God has in store for me? Your position isn't just related to your physical state, but also your mental state based on how you see yourself. Consider how Gideon thinks of himself. He tells the angel of the Lord, "My clan is the weakest in Manasseh, and I am the least in my family" (Judges 6:15). The angel responded to Gideon and informed him that he is a mighty warrior! Often, we count ourselves out of what God is calling us to do simply because of our circumstances. If you could only see how God thinks of you! How many times have you delayed what God is calling you to do simply because of your current situation? Common phrases such as, "*I don't have enough money*" and "*I don't have the qualifications*" are used as excuses to make us settle with our current position in life. It is time for you to change your mindset! God put you in your current situation because it is intended to serve a unique purpose for His plan in your life.

Don't look at what you don't have! Look at God! Gideon starts out with thousands of men in his army but defeats the Midianites with only three hundred. God can do a lot with a little. The Lord tells Gideon, "You have too many men. I cannot deliver Midian into their hands, or Israel would boast against me, 'My own strength has saved me'" (Judges 7:2). God is the same with us. If God gave us all of the resources initially, then many of us would walk around, taking all the credit for our success. God puts us through struggles in life to give us a reason to rely on Him. Once you are successful,

> God provides your blessings in the place that He expects you to be.

then you will be able to reflect and see God's impact. God wants to walk with us daily on our journey to understanding our purpose. He walked with Enoch faithfully for over 300 years, so why wouldn't He walk with you?

Take a snapshot of your current situation: your finances, job status, marriage, etc. Look at all the things that God has already blessed you with! The same God is ready to take you to the next level in life. It's time to shift your perspective and start telling yourself *"All I have is all I need!"* Start planning like the business has taken off! Save and invest your money like your current balance is exactly where you want it to be. Use whatever you have and begin to work towards your purpose! God honors your perseverance! Your willingness to trust Him will accelerate your path towards your purpose in life. You are built for purpose! Whatever you don't have, God will provide it for you! Paul writes in Romans 8:28, "And we know that all things work together for the good of those who love the Lord and are called according to His purpose." Meaning that as long as you walk into God's purpose for your life, He will work everything out.

Think about the story of Joseph in Genesis. The story of Joseph highlights many different areas of activating your purpose. As a young boy, Joseph has a set of dreams where God gave him a snapshot of his future. Joseph immediately relays the dreams to his father and brothers. As you could imagine, his family is overcome with a mixture of confusion and jealousy. The brothers conspire to get rid of Joseph. The brothers sell him to the Ishmaelites where he ends up in Egypt. As a slave, Joseph endures betrayal multiple times, false allegations, and an entire famine before his original dreams come to pass. If God included all of the sufferings in the dream, would Joseph have been so eager to pursue His purpose? Absolutely not! The struggle was necessary because it anchored Joseph's heart in God. Like Joseph, I know many of you have struggled with asking God why. *Why can't I get that promotion? Why hasn't my business taken off? Why am I still not married?* You must remember God's timing is not equivalent to our timing.

Joseph spent many years in the same location. During his wait, God was working on the things around Joseph. Joseph's wait allowed God to work. Joseph became the answer to Pharaoh's problems. He not only was freed from prison but also rose in command. So Joseph's posture led to his freedom AND elevation. A proper posture while waiting is one of the most important things that God wants you to have before He blesses you. Your waiting posture serves a unique purpose because it allows God to see that you are reliant on Him. You must be willing to operate in His timing. In the meantime, God begins to work on your behalf, and once you get into position, the Bible says that He will "restore to us the years" that you've felt you may have lost (Joel 2:25).

During your wait, I want to inform you that the enemy understands that your name is the subject of many supernatural conversations. The enemy knows you can change the entire world with God's calling for your life. Therefore, the enemy uses worldly things to distract you from purpose. Let's fast forward to the book of Job. From the beginning of the chapter, we see that God is having a cosmic conversation with the enemy. He uses Job to show the enemy an example of someone who is "blameless and upright" (Job 1:8). The enemy used the people and things around Job to try and steal his commitment to God. If Job would have turned away from God, he would've been blinded from his purpose. Similarly, know that

God's timing is not equivalent to our timing.

the enemy will use people and things that you're connected to as a detour from God's purpose.

Job had faith and sought answers from God. God rewards him with more than he ever lost. Why? Job kept his focus on God. The attacks that you have faced or are facing have purpose behind them. God will never put you through something that He cannot deliver you from. Attacks from the enemy are inevitable, it comes with walking in purpose.

Additionally, consistent attacks should sound an alarm in your head, as a cue that you are walking in God's purpose. The enemy will do whatever he can to block you from God's purpose for your life. Can I share a secret with you? The enemy is nervous about your purpose. Your business, relationships, or whatever you may be building has the power to change the world. Activating it will not only affect you, but generations after you. No wonder the enemy is so committed to distracting you from purpose!

I've had internal and external battles that hindered me from purpose, but God guided me through multiple stories in the Bible to help me understand my purpose. The stories that we will dissect are the necessary ingredients to help you live a purposeful life. This book is intended to help you walk into the purpose that God has set for your life. We will spend the next chapters analyzing people who endured uncomfortable situations in order to activate their purpose. Since God has given each of us unique skill sets, your purpose may look different. This means that the path to activate purpose is much different for each person. Building your relationship with God will help you understand the way that He has set out for you.

The enemy is nervous about your purpose.

We must go and get everything God has for us. A lot of today's books teach this "hustle and grind" mentality. However, issues occur because people chase after their desires instead of what God desires. The result of chasing after our own desires is a continuous state of confusion with no true fulfillment in life. Conversely, receiving what God has will help us be completely healed and fulfilled.

Activate Your Purpose is designed to point you in the direction of your purpose. I don't want to make any promises by saying, *"After reading this you will know exactly what to do with your life!"* Frankly, the only book that can do that is the Bible. However, my hope is that this book will help with your endurance as you search for purpose. You will then begin to understand why things are happening around you and how it relates to your overall purpose in life.

Understand this...your purpose is bigger than you. It is much more than you envision. There is something on the inside of you that is waiting to be unraveled. Think about Jacob, on the inside of him was Israel. An entire nation that is still present today. Talk about purpose! Jacob had to be in the right place to understand what was inside of him. More importantly, he had to wrestle to bring it out. Finding purpose is not easy, it requires work! It requires you to overcome one of the biggest giants...yourself. It also requires you to sacrifice your own wants and desires. This allows your life to be a living sacrifice to God. God puts many people through seasons of struggle in order to find purpose. You are no different. On the other side of their struggles, God rewards His servants for their faithfulness and obedience. God wants to reward you as well!

This book is for the next generation of leaders. Yes, you are a leader. No matter your industry or background this book will help you to understand how God has used people to activate purpose. You will gain insight into how God may be intending to use you in this season. Whatever you may be going through, remember God has a purpose for you. God gives it to us, but it is necessary for us to receive it. This is why the Bible talks about the Israelites going to "possess the land" (Num 33:53, Joshua 1:11). God gave the Israelites the Promised Land, but it was their responsibility to go and possess it. I mentioned earlier in the introduction that Abraham was known formerly as Abram. This is significant because it wasn't just about a name change but God was also changing his mindset. I believe that God is shifting your mindset from "Abram" to "Abraham" right now. It is time for you to think bigger! This means you must walk AND possess everything God has planned for your life.

Your purpose is valuable to the kingdom! It is crucial that you understand and receive it! I pray that as you walk into your purpose that things begin to shift. The obstacles in your life are only meant for you to activate whatever God is calling for you. Don't run from your problems, get through them! The reward is worth the pain. This is your opportunity to walk into the promises God has for you. Throughout these chapters, there will be stories that help you to grow. Let's go. Ready...set...ACTIVATE!

Thought: Activation is the stage before usage. God wants you to activate your purpose, and then He will begin to show you His desires for your life.

2

The Help

In 2011, the movie, The Help was released. The film focuses on the plight of African-American housemaids during the 1960s. Aibileen, played by Viola Davis, was persuaded by a white journalist named Eugenia, otherwise known as "Skeeter," to document her treatment as a housemaid. Aibileen also persuaded her fellow housemaids to give accounts of their struggles. I love the movie because it shows the severity of the housemaids' struggles while also showing the relationship between their work and the Civil Rights movement. I started thinking about the biblical significance of the film. One day, God spoke to me saying, "Purpose requires sacrifice." I reflected on the movie, and it all came to me at once that this movie was about one key thing... sacrifice.

For those who have not seen this movie, I won't spoil it for you. However, there are a couple of points that I want to make that will help you understand how this movie relates to activating your purpose. On one side, Aibileen and the rest of the housemaids sacrifice their lives communicating with Skeeter about their experiences. During this period in history, it was dangerous for African-

Americans to communicate with Caucasians, especially attempting to write a book together. Aibileen's friend, Minnie, even sacrifices her own marriage taking a stand against her treatment as a housemaid. On the other side, we see Skeeter making a sacrifice of her own by writing and publishing the book for the housemaids. She sacrifices relationships in her life and even social status to help improve the housemaids' condition.

The theme of sacrifice is evident throughout the movie. The sacrifices of all the women ultimately work out for both parties. I believe that this movie is not just intended to make us historically aware of the housemaids' treatment in the 1960s. More so, I think it serves as an indicator of how God intends for us to live. One of the lessons learned from the movie is that to create change we must sacrifice. The women's overall purpose was to create a better life for African-Americans. Likewise, our purpose is realized through sacrifice.

I know that there have been times in your life where you have been like, "How do I find what I am called to do?" Many hours of prayer and self-help books, and you are still confused about your calling. It's okay! We have all been there. Sometimes the problem in life isn't with our methods. It is our focus! Whenever our focus is not aligned with God, it creates confusion. One of the things that God values the most is relationships. If you don't believe it, look at the story of Creation. God took time to walk with Adam through the garden in order to build their relationship. Adam understands what he is called to do because of his relationship with God. Adam's commitment to God's assignment ultimately allows him to get the thing he most desired, Eve.

Helping others requires sacrifice. Adam submits to God before he gets what he desires. The same thing is true in your life. Sacrifice looks different for everyone, but it is necessary for everyone. Let's look into how Jesus tells an expert in the law how sacrifice is needed to inherit eternal life.

We can all agree that our life's main purpose is getting into Heaven. In Luke 10, a certain lawyer asks Jesus how to inherit eternal life. Jesus proceeds to tell him a story that is famously known as "The Good Samaritan." Jesus illustrates the narrative: "A man was going down from Jerusalem to Jericho, when he was attacked by robbers. They stripped him of his clothes, beat him and went away, leaving him half dead" (Luke 10:30). One man was a priest, and the other was a Levite (Levites worked for the church). The people that you would expect to help the man were the very ones that passed him over. Theologians believe that the priest and the Levite passed over the man because he would've been considered unclean. Too often have we allowed religion to hinder us from purpose. People use religion as a reason not to associate with certain people or go places. Sometimes, God intends for us to go to those very places to be the help for someone in need.

Becoming attached to the law and religion could cause you to miss the thing God is actually telling you to do. We see this when God sent Jesus to Earth to save mankind. The Gospels provide a snapshot of how much the Pharisees were attached to many Old Testament beliefs. They distanced themselves from many lepers, adulterers, and other "sinners" in the Bible. Sadly, we often have the same mentality as the Pharisees. Conversely, Jesus' mission was to go to the areas and be the help for people who needed to be healed.

Despite the rejection, there was one who helped the beaten man. The one who helped was a Samaritan. The town of Samaria was mixed with Israelites and people of foreign descent. The background information is crucial because the Jewish people did not accept the people of Samaria. They worshipped the same God, but practiced their faith differently. The difference in practice caused

> People use religion as a reason to not associate with certain people or go places, but God may intend for you to go back and help those you previously left behind.

Jewish people to despise both their ethnicity and religion. The Jews had been against the Samaritans for hundreds of years. How ironic is it that the Samaritan helps the injured man? Jesus strategically uses a Samaritan to show that one of the key components of love is compassion. Take a moment and think about all of the people that have either betrayed, laughed, or talked about you. Now imagine if they were injured, would you stop what you were doing to help them? If your answer is no, then you must fix your posture! Why? Purpose requires sacrifice. Many of us are in search of purpose but are unwilling to make any kind of sacrifice.

The Good Samaritan allows us to understand key points to activate purpose. The first step of activating your purpose is to sacrifice your time. Whenever Jesus introduces the Samaritan in the story, He says that the Samaritan was traveling "somewhere." There are many times in life where we travel - people travel to a store, job, and all other kinds of destinations. How many times have you seen a person in need while traveling? Most of us have our own schedule, and any aberration in those plans we often ignore. We see people on the street and say to ourselves, *"Someone else will help them"* or *"I am running late"* to cope with ignoring them. Is this you? Frequently we see this, even in church! One example is whenever we circumscribe tithes and offerings to just money. Tithing is not just about money; it deals with our actions as well. Don't limit your offerings to just money, it is more about your lifestyle! God is concerned with our hearts more than our bank accounts.

A lot of people want their lives to change but are unwilling to change their lives.

Let's look at Abraham's test with Isaac. God assigns Abraham to go to the top of the mountain and sacrifice his son, the son that he has been waiting for his entire life. After following God to the mountain, we learned that God never intended for Abraham to sacrifice his son. God had a ram prepared for him! God just wanted to know Abraham's heart by examining his willingness to sacrifice something so precious to him. What is your "Isaac?" It could represent your schedule. Why? Time is the most precious thing that we all have on Earth. Our time is more important than anything. Remember whenever God asks you to sacrifice, it is usually something that is precious to you!

Many people today have the same mindset as the priest and Levite. They pass over people in need, just because of an unwillingness to sacrifice time. We associate any aberration to our plans as a waste of time. However, our purpose is usually in the very place that leads us askew. Think about Paul on the road to Damascus. Paul's journey takes a sudden turn, and it changes the course of his life forever. God had to stop Paul on his original path, completely transforming his life. The sacrifice of your time is not meant for God, but it is intended for you. The waiting in your life allows you to realize that purpose is not on our timing but instead God's.

Next, activating your purpose happens when you sacrifice your position. Jesus tells the audience that the Samaritan not only stops what he was doing, but he "came to where the man was; and when he saw him, he took pity on him" (Luke 10:33). The Samaritan "coming to where the man was" is not just about meeting him physically, but he also met the injured man where he was spiritually. God has assigned for us to be the help in both realms. In life, you will encounter people with different beliefs or varying degrees of spiritual maturity. We must get down from our "high horse." Whenever we stay in that self-elevated position, we become just like the Pharisees.

Jesus wants us to truly meet people where they are. Meeting people where they are consists of getting down from our current position to help save those who are lost. Understand, this does not mean lessening your morals and values to appease people. You must continue to carry yourself with high standards but be willing to reach everyone. God places us in situations where we have to sacrifice our current state. Jesus became a servant and so should you. Having the heart of a servant keeps you from being a prude Christian. Sacrificing your position means that you must get uncomfortable, go into environments, and meet whoever needs help just like the Samaritan. We assume that the man the Samaritan helps was just physically hurt, but there could have been mental and spiritual hurt as well. There are also times that the enemy has robbed us of things supernaturally. You have probably been in the same position as the wounded man where the enemy has robbed you of your happiness, joy, and peace. There are actually more people in this world, more than you think, who have been robbed both naturally and supernaturally.

Similar to the Samaritan, God is positioning you to be "The Help" to those who are hurting. He has equipped you with all of the resources and skills needed to save those who are suffering physically and spiritually. The Samaritan puts the man on his own donkey and carries him to a local inn. The same donkey that takes the Samaritan to a certain point was meant to carry someone else at another point. Sometimes, the resources that God has given us in one season are meant to help others in another season.

> Sometimes, the resources that God has given us in one season
> are meant to help others in another season.

We have seen the Samaritan sacrifice his time and position. The last sacrifice that must be made is sacrificing a reward. Huh? Let's continue with the story of the Samaritan. The Samaritan carries the injured man on his donkey to a local inn. When they arrive, the Samaritan pays for his stay and tells the innkeeper, "and when I return, I will reimburse you for any extra expense you may have" (Luke 10:35). So let's recap the Samaritan's day so far: he gives up his plans, then gives up his own donkey, and now he spends money for the man to have a place to stay. Jesus never says that the injured man tells the Samaritan thank you, nor does He say that the Samaritan ever asks for his money back. Our society today is drenched in capitalism, where we have to profit on everything that we do. I'd imagine a handful of people would have their CashApp requests ready to send in order to get their money back. The Bible says, "For the Son of Man is going to come in the glory of His Father with His angels, and will then repay every man according to his deeds" (Matt. 16:27). Oftentimes, God wants you to sacrifice a physical reward from people because He will then reward you in more ways than you can imagine.

Many of you are probably asking if this book's goal is to activate my own purpose in life, then why does the book start with helping others? Growing up, before I would be able to get anything I wanted I had to do my chores around the house. I had a role to play in our household's overall well-being. The same thing is true with the Kingdom. God wants you to take part in His overall purpose on Earth. Our purpose on Earth is to love others. In order to activate our individual purpose, it is important to show to our Heavenly Father that we can handle the responsibility with His overall purpose. We never know where the Samaritan was traveling to originally. I believe God was leading the Samaritan to the injured man the whole time! What the Samaritan might have thought was a detour, God saw it as purpose. God knew that there was an injured man that needed help, and He also knew the traveling Samaritan that was the answer. Oftentimes, whenever we pray to God, we are the ones asking Him for help. *God, please help me with this test. Help me with my relationship.* However, what if we shift our focus by asking God, "*How can I help others?*" God has equipped you to be an answer for the world. He has given you unique skills and abilities to help someone else. Even Batman has a Robin! God has prepared you to be the "Robin" for someone special and has prepared a "Robin" for you! When God created Eve from the rib of Adam, He created her for a specific purpose to serve as the "suitable helper" for Adam, and to carry on mankind's purpose on Earth. Eve was created to be an answer. YOU were created to be an answer!

How to be The Help

The question now is how does this apply to me? If you are still feeling confused, I want to provide you with a couple of ways that you can be a blessing to others. These lessons are things that I have been taught from leaders in my own life and believe that it can help you as well.

1. 10 Minute Rule

This one is straightforward. Each day take around 10 minutes to think about someone special in your life. During that time, focus on why they are special to you. Step out of your comfort zone and tell them why they are special. Call them. Text them. Maybe even write them a note and send it to them. This allows you to focus more on people and less on yourself. You would be amazed by how uplifting this message can be to a person's life. Also, this works whenever you may be down because it allows you to see the relationships that you have cultivated throughout your journey in life. Can't think of anyone? Think about the one who has never changed, God. Think about His goodness and mercy and the many times He has delivered you. The 10-minute rule is a great way to start your morning. It gives you the ability to remove yourself from the equation and fixes your mindset to focus on people.

2. Be a Blessing Today

One of my friends came to me excited while we were working on homework. He said, *"Bro guess what? I was at Starbucks this morning, and the guy in front of me paid for my order!"* I laughed because he was overcome with excitement. It was almost 5 hours after the man blessed him with the coffee, and it was still at the top of his mind. That small gesture stuck with him that long, and he is probably even still thinking about it! Why can't that be you? Take time to be a blessing to someone today. It may not necessarily be paying for someone's coffee, but maybe it could be holding the door for someone. These things may seem small for some, but it is significant for others. The thing I love about the story is that my friend looks at me and says, *"I was thinking to myself if I should pay for the guy behind me."* That blessed me so much! What it showed was the impact of a blessing. Helping others has a contagious effect. The beauty of it is if you take the time to be a blessing to someone today, it can potentially affect the entire world tomorrow.

3. Let It GO

For me, this is probably the hardest one of all. It is in our human nature to win. This is why every show you see today is some sort of competition. I love to win. I always like winning the argument or getting the last word. Wanting to win is beneficial, but in some ways, can also be detrimental. The problem with wanting to win is that sometimes it comes at the expense of relationships along with peace and happiness. Check to see if pride has gotten in the way of any relationship in your life. If so, you need to communicate and address those issues. There will always be times where you may "lose" an argument or want to say something back. Remember to value the relationship more than any argument.

4. Let Love Lead

Sometimes right is not always right. I know you read that and said, "Huh?" It's okay, I will explain. See, the Levite and the priest were both right based on the law leaving the injured man because he was considered unclean. However, the Samaritan did what was right in the eyes of Jesus. His judgment was not based on doctrine, but on love. There are times in our life where we look to do everything right, and according to the script. However, most of life happens off-script. The question is, what is your response when life throws things at you? God sends Jesus to the Earth because everything was happening based on a script. The Pharisees led with doctrine, but Jesus led with love. It is crucial that in our lives that we have a heart for people. All of our decisions and actions should be centered around love. That way, "The Help" goes from what you do and becomes who you are.

* * *

What's the Big Idea?

Whenever Jesus talks about the greatest commandment in Matthew 22, He replies, "Love the Lord your God with all your heart and with all your soul and with all your mind." Jesus then replies and says, "And the second is like it: "'Love your neighbor as yourself" (Matthew 22:39). Jesus shows that in order to abide by God's law you must first love Him, and then love others. Many people struggle to find purpose in life because they focus so much on themselves instead of focusing on others. However, God allows us to find purpose through other people. In order to truly love another person, it means that we have to give something. John 3:16 states, "For God so loved the world that he gave his one and only Son, that whoever believes in him shall not perish but have eternal life." So God shows us how to love by giving His Son to save us from sin. Jesus restores God's purpose for mankind. In order to activate your purpose, it is crucial that your focus is to give first, so that you may receive His blessing for you. Throughout the Bible, Jesus serves as "The Help" in many different situations. There is one situation in particular that highlights Jesus serving others.

In Luke 9, after preaching about fasting, a synagogue leader comes to Jesus because His daughter has died. As Jesus goes to heal the man's daughter, something miraculous happens. A woman comes through the crowd and touches His cloak. The woman had been "subject to bleeding" for 12 years. Struggling with her health issues, the woman probably struggled with her faith. The woman's days were probably filled with rejection from local doctors, and she also spent all of her money.... suffering AND broke. What a combination! No one could endure that for a day, let alone more than a decade! With nowhere left to turn she does what all of us should do, she turns to Jesus.

If you wonder how to be "The Help" look at Jesus' response.

1. U CAN Touch This

In 2012, former President Barack Obama came to Florence, SC, as a stop on his campaign trail. Since this was in my hometown, my father and I made it a mission to go and see him. We understood the gravity of this moment. Obama had the opportunity to make history as the first Black American President. In order for this to happen, my dad and I waited outside of the Civic Center for hours. The line wrapped around the building almost twice. It was amazing to see everyone excited to be a part of history. After hours of waiting, we finally entered the building. Music was playing along with people discussing their own political stances. As a kid, I had no clue what these people were talking about. I was only concerned with seeing President Obama. Finally, the moment came as people cheered all over the building. What amazed me the most was what happened at the end of the event. After President Obama spoke, he went around the entire building to greet people. Crowds gathered and reached their hands out just to touch him. I was fortunate to have the opportunity to shake his hand and I still remember the moment vividly. Thinking back on this moment, it is interesting how I don't remember anything he said that night, but I do remember shaking his hand. I am certain that there were many other people who felt the same way that night!

I believe the reason President Obama gained so much notoriety wasn't just because of what he said, but because of what he did. Many celebrities that night would've probably left after the event was over, but Obama was different than any other celebrity. He allowed people to touch him. There wasn't a barrage of security surrounding him. That one moment made him feel normal to everyone in that room. It made him feel approachable, therefore, people were willing to vote for him. As a leader, this is a lesson that you must learn. You must be willing to let others touch you. Not necessarily physical touch, more so you must allow yourself to be vulnerable with people you are leading. In the Bible, we see the woman physically touching Jesus. However, I believe that through her touching Jesus' garment, she touches His heart.

Jesus was actually on His way to perform another miracle whenever the woman stops Him. Jesus and the disciples probably had a schedule set for the day. However, Jesus was willing to alter His schedule for those in need of help. The woman touching Jesus probably acted out of character barging through the crowd in order to touch Jesus. She was desperate for a miracle and knew that He was the only one who could heal her. Maybe God has equipped you with the skills and abilities to be the answer to someone else's problem. In order to be The Help, you must first be approachable. The woman saw Jesus' willingness to associate with the common people. This probably gave her the courage to go and reach out to Him. People can only reach out to you if you are reachable! Obama was willing to ignore his schedule and associate with us into the night. The stories that he heard that night probably helped build the platforms on which he was running. If you ignore people, you may be ignoring purpose!

2. Hide and Go Seek

When the woman touches Jesus, He instantly asks, "Who touched me?" At first, you are probably like "uh oh." If someone said this today, you would automatically think that these are "fighting words." However, Jesus was interested to find the woman who touched Him. Jesus could have easily kept going to His intended destination without trying to figure out who touched His garment. Many of us would have probably ignored her gesture and continued about our day. Peter even tells Jesus, "Master, the people are crowding and pressing against you." (Luke 8:45). So, it would have been

If you ignore people, you may be ignoring purpose!

easier for Jesus to go forward instead of turning around and fighting through the crowd.

Jesus not only "leaves the ninety-nine for the one" (Matthew 18:12), but I believe He also fights through the ninety-nine to get to the one. Not, literal fighting of course. More so, He is willing to chase after us even if it means getting through a crowded area. In the same way, we must be willing to leave the crowd to help those in need. Many people get lost in the "crowds" in life. For you, the crowd might represent a large social media presence. Jesus was willing to leave what was popular for what was right. There may be some things God is calling you to that may not be popular, even to those closest to you. Remember, Peter was insisting that Jesus keep going. However, Jesus knew that there was unfinished business. Even if He would have gone forward, He probably would have still been thinking about the woman in the back of His mind. Therefore, Jesus had to find the woman who needed Him.

A popular childhood game is hide and go seek. No need to explain the rules of the game because I am sure you have played it as well. In life, we tend to play this game more often than we think. It may not be for the joy of playing the game, but it may happen with people that see inadequacies within themselves. What do I mean? In middle school, there was a guy in my class who was always quiet. He never would talk to anyone and would always isolate himself. One day, my friends and I decided to talk with him to see why he was so quiet. In about five minutes, he instantly became one of our friends. The reason he was so quiet was that he had a speech impediment. He assumed that this would be a turnoff to a lot of people. For him to feel important we had to go seek him. You may be faced with a

> Jesus was willing to leave what was popular for what was right.

similar situation in your life right now. There are people that need you but are hiding from you! To help them you must seek them.

3. Patience is a Virtue

Once Jesus returns to the woman with the issue of blood, she nervously approaches Him trembling. The woman probably was nervous because she believed Jesus was about to reprimand her for touching Him. Jesus stood before her and listened to the woman as she told Him the truth about what happened. What is interesting is that Jesus already knew her entire story before she was even born. However, Jesus still takes time to listen to her story. I believe what Jesus shows us is that love is shown through patience. How many times have you been around somebody who you were halfway listening to? The reason is that you just didn't care that much. This is something that I have an issue with so don't feel bad! However, in order to be "The Help," you must care about the ones you are helping.

Jesus in this instance is aware that listening to the woman is not for Him, but more so for herself. Jesus' patience allows the woman not only to tell people around her the issues she had but also how Jesus fixed them. Now don't think that Jesus came back to boast about His own power. The concern of the woman was not about why the issue was gone, but it was about how it happened. Jesus says to her, "Daughter, be of good comfort: thy faith hath made thee whole; go in peace" (Luke 8:48). This is why Jesus had to come back after she touched Him. She was healed, but not whole! Just because you help someone with their issues doesn't mean they are whole. Jesus had to come back so that she wouldn't get herself back into the same situation again. You have to constantly check up on the people that you are called to help! Think back to the story of the Good Samaritan. He made an effort not only to help the man, but he returns to check on him (Luke 10:35). Your patience with others will help make them whole. Healing from the outside can happen instantly, but healing on the inside requires time.

Remember that patience and waiting are two different things. Patience is your posture while you wait. Your posture is the position of your heart. Check to see if your heart's content with trusting in all of God's plans for your life. Even while waiting. Everyone has to wait for something, but everyone is not patient. As you deal with people in your life, you must be patient. There will be many people that will listen to you then turn and get themselves back into the same situation. Whenever Jesus leaves, we don't know what the woman does after. It was not important because Jesus would have done it as many times as He needed in order for the woman to be made whole! You have to trust in God with the healing process. Whenever you get discouraged with people, remember how hard it was for you to change! This way you can have compassion for others and their situations. God honors your patience! As you continue to help others, God will position you with more responsibility. Once He trusts you to be The Help with one person, you will be amazed about the opportunities He presents you with. Remember, "Whoever can be trusted with very little can also be trusted with much" (Luke 16:10). There is a big "Help Wanted" sign on this world and God is waiting for you to go and change people's lives.

In your life, change comes with sacrifice. Reaching any goal in your life requires sacrifices. Activating your purpose is dependent on your sacrifices. Not just for yourself but also for others. When you think about any situation in your life, ask yourself, "What is the

Patience is your posture while you wait.

focus?" If it is strictly on you, it must change and become centered around God and His people.

Thought: Sacrifice is crucial in any relationship. In your relationship with God AND your relationship with people. The steps to finding the purpose that God has for you are all dependent on your sacrifices to Him and how you treat His people.

3

Designated Deliverer

In college, there are many different job opportunities students can have. There are work-study jobs, tutoring, and fast food jobs available. One of the more interesting jobs that are in high demand, especially in college towns, is a designated driver.

A designated driver's responsibility is to remain sober and transport people, who may or may not be under the influence of drugs or alcohol, to a specific location. The people who are under the influence trust and rely on the designated driver to carry them to their desired destination. In the meantime, the riders enjoy the rest of their night. Due to laws centered around safety, companies like Uber and Lyft have profited by providing a platform for designated drivers around the world. Despite its popularity, being a designated driver is a tall task! I bet that designated drivers have heard a lot of interesting things while driving people to parties, clubs, and even home.

It is not only the responsibility of the designated driver to make sure people get from point A to point B, but also to take care of them while they are under the influence. Protecting them from things like alcohol poisoning, saying the wrong thing, or messing with the wrong person. Designated drivers understand that the people they are transporting are more than likely acting out of character.

So why am I talking about drinking in a book about the Bible and purpose? Well, here it is... God sometimes appoints people in our lives to serve as the designated driver to carry us into our purpose.

Confused? Yeah, I figured.

Let me explain. Naturally, we think of this person as a "designated driver," but spiritually we must look at them as a "designated deliverer." These are people that lay down their lives to help others achieve what God has set for His people. This is why God appoints prophets. Prophets spend most of their lives learning the voice of God and most of their work happens where no one sees. Like a designated driver, we would probably consider that responsibility boring. Prophets get to spend their entire lives interceding and pleading for the sake of others.

Think about Moses, one of the most notable prophets in the Bible. God calls Moses down from the mountain in order to free the Hebrew people from Egypt. Moses barely even knows the Hebrew people; however, God saw it fit for Moses to lead them into the Promised Land. God calls Moses from a high place. The high place represents the comfortable areas in your life. God had to take Moses from where he was comfortable and make him uncomfortable. Moses had to plead with Pharaoh to free the Hebrew people ten different times. Once they were freed and in the wilderness, Moses had to endure people complaining about the wilderness, people worshipping false idols, and even his own family turning against him. However, Moses still goes to the mountain and pleads for God not to kill the people for their wrongdoings. He asks God to feed and nourish the people whenever they complain. In addition, there

God sometimes appoints people in our lives to serve as the designated driver to carry us into our purpose.

are long periods of waiting that Moses endures on the mountain waiting to hear from God for guidance and direction. He never even gets to go into the Promised Land and still has to lead the Israelites through the wilderness. So Moses' entire life was to serve people. God has to make Moses uncomfortable because he is called to be a deliverer.

Moses had to lead a people that weren't necessarily physically drunk but more so spiritually drunk. For hundreds of years, they had to consume the beliefs and traditions of the Egyptians. Many generations had passed since Joseph had come into Egypt. The people were not familiar with the God of Israel. Even Moses himself had to be introduced to God through a burning bush on the mountain. Moses asks God how he should refer to Him whenever he speaks to the people. God tells Moses, "'I AM WHO I AM. This is what you are to say to the Israelites: 'I AM has sent me to you" (Exodus 3:14). Moses' question shows that he would have to introduce the Hebrew people to God as well. Even until the Red Sea the Israelites were still learning about God. When the people saw what God did with the Red Sea "the people feared the LORD" and "believed in the LORD" (Exodus 14:31).

Fast forward to the golden calf. Moses comes down from the mountain with the Ten Commandments in his hand. Once he comes down, he sees the Israelites worshipping a golden calf. Moses was livid! Out of anger he throws the tablets that were in his hand on the ground and breaks them. If the Israelites knew God, why would they be worshipping a golden calf? The golden calf was a product of their drunkenness from the things they consumed in

Egypt. The golden calf was a symbol from one of the Egyptian gods. On the quest to the Promised Land, some of the Hebrew people wanted to go back to Egypt. The Israelites were so consumed with their old way of life that they became "drunk" to that lifestyle. The slave mentality had intoxicated them so much, they were unsure what it was like to be free. They kept looking back at Egypt so much that it took their eyes from the Promised Land that God had for them. This is why God allowed for the children to be the ones to enter the Promised Land because there had to be a fresh and sober mindset walking into the new places.

Take note of this. There are times we have to understand that there are things that God is waiting to give us that have been stalled simply because He is waiting on us to release the old things. This is why Jesus says, "And no one pours new wine into old wineskins. Otherwise, the wine will burst the skins, and both the wine and the wineskins will be ruined. No, they pour new wine into new wineskins" (Mark 2:22). Change in your life starts with a mindset shift! Understand that your dream spouse may have not been introduced to you yet simply because you're still drunk from that old toxic relationship. Stop focusing on all the things that you have lost. Sometimes you can become so "intoxicated" with rejection that you miss new opportunities. Focus on what God is preparing you for in the next season! The enemy's strategy in the wilderness is to intoxicate you. The enemy shows Jesus in the wilderness "all the kingdoms of the world and their splendor" (Matthew 4:8) because his goal was for Jesus to get drunk with power and status. Jesus remained sober by reflecting on God's word instead of the enemy's lies.

You can sometimes even get drunk from religion. Now before you close this book, I want you to understand I am not saying don't go to church or read your Bible. No, the Bible tells us to meditate on God's word (Psalm 1:2). However, understand that God is not constrained to the Bible. God has the power to work outside of His own

> The slave mentality has intoxicated them so much, they were
> unsure what it was like to be free.

Law. Jesus shows us this when He talks to the Samaritan woman at the well, performing miracles on the Sabbath, and saves an adulterer from getting stoned. The Pharisees plotted to kill Jesus because He was changing people's perspectives on the Law. It's crucial that you don't miss Jesus because you are too focused on doctrine. Think how many more miracles Jesus could have performed if people's mindsets weren't limited? How can we limit God to normal when He is supernatural? Don't get intoxicated with normal! You are intoxicated with normal whenever you think thoughts like *"nobody like me can get this kind of job"* and *"this is how it always has been."* A "normal mindset" limits our perspective on what God can do.

Stop letting where you come from determine where you go. Jesus didn't let his environment stop Him. Nathanael, a follower of Jesus, says, "Can anything good come from Nazareth?" (John 1:46). We see people already limited Jesus simply because of where He came from. That didn't stop Jesus, and neither should it stop you! The enemy tries to make you look at your past, your current situation, and your environments as barriers.

However, God wants to use you as an example to break those pre-established barriers. Don't get drunk dwelling on your current situation, it is only the enemy trying to distract you from purpose! Instead think, *"God what are you teaching me while I am in this situation?"* God may have called you to be the deliverer for your environment. God may be using you to be an example for that boss that makes you despise your job. He may be using your struggle to motivate others. The truth is that YOU may be the only Jesus some people ever see! That is why God will put you in situations to help you be the deliverer for those who don't yet know Him.

In order to further show this concept of the designated deliverer, let's jump to one of my favorite stories in the Bible found in the book of Ruth. However, we are not talking about Ruth nor Boaz. In church, we have spent many Women's Day services talking about these two, but we miss one crucial woman in the story that God uses, Naomi.

For those who aren't familiar with the story. Bethlehem was in the midst of a famine. We see from the beginning of the chapter that Naomi is faced with adversity. In response to the famine, Naomi and her family traveled to Moab in search of a new life. There is an important lesson right here. God often makes us uncomfortable so that we can go to the place He desires for us. God will purposefully put us through a famine in order to position us for what He intends to do.

Naomi arrives in Moab and her husband dies all of a sudden. Not only that, but her own two sons also die in Moab! After all the men in her life died, she is left with the widows of her two sons, Ruth and Orpah. Naomi decides to go back to Bethlehem because she thinks there is no purpose for her in Moab. Orpah decides to stay, but Ruth chooses to go with Naomi to Bethlehem. God places Naomi in Moab temporarily in order to be the designated deliverer for Ruth.

Traveling to Purpose

Ruth urges Naomi to carry her along whenever she decides to go back to Bethlehem. See Ruth was from Moab. Whenever talking about a Moabite, it's crucial to jump all the way back to Genesis. We know that Moabites originate from Lot and his daughters. The inception of the Moabite lineage begins while Lot is drunk (Gen-

Stop letting where you come from determine where you go.

esis 19:33). How ironic! The generations of Moabites were filled with incest, adultery, and worshipping other gods. The Moabites opposed the Israelites for many years. This means Ruth was not aware of the God of Israel! It was not Ruth's fault for the lineage she was born into. However, Ruth didn't let that hinder her from the ability to live a better life. Take note this applies to your life as well! You may have been born with a disadvantage. However, society's stereotypes don't determine the trajectory of your future. Remember, relationships are important to God. Relationships are what reflect His image! As you are being delivered, you may also become the deliverer for someone else.

God wanted to use Ruth as the example to carry His purpose, but He uses Naomi to help activate Ruth's purpose. Naomi goes through so much adversity. She loses her home, her husband, and her sons. What a tough situation! However, in the midst of her adversity, something so profound occurs. Naomi tells Ruth to go with her sister Orpah but look at Ruth's response. Ruth says, "Don't urge me to leave you or to turn back from you. Where you go I will go, and where you stay I will stay. Your people will be my people and your God my God" (Ruth 1:16). So in the midst of Naomi's adversity, Ruth could still see God in her. This shows that Naomi remained faithful to God in the midst of her hardships.

Like Naomi, many of us probably wonder why God puts us in certain situations. Part of being a designated deliverer is not just being a deliverer physically, but also spiritually. People must be able to see God in you through good and bad times. Naomi's spiritual walk inspired Ruth! Your spiritual journey can have the same effect! There are people around you that see the way you carry yourself and that is ultimately how they view Christianity. This is why Jesus' walk was so effective. Jesus was able to change the hearts of many because His love never changed. The same love God gives us is the same we must give to the world! An important principle to remember is that to effectively carry others into purpose you must first carry yourself in the way that God desires.

You may even be the designated deliverer for people you may never encounter! Think about Rev. Dr. Martin Luther King Jr. He risks his entire life to help a generation of people he would never get to see. Many quotes and ideas have been taken from Dr. King simply because of the way he walked. People see him as a civil rights activist, or speaker, but remember he was first a Christian preacher! Even through his death, he was able to deliver a people out of a racist and prejudiced Jim Crow era and inspire future generations to push forward towards equality. Think on this. Both Dr. King and Naomi were able to endure profound adversity because they were centered in Christ. Even though Naomi had one person following her and Dr. King had millions, both were impactful and carried people into purpose. Neither Naomi nor Dr. King needed any form of social media to help build their following. Their faith in God alone brought the right people to them! I am not saying don't utilize social media. All I am saying is that they did not have to rely on any platform on social media to get followers. The point is that God assigns the right people to follow you once you follow Him.

So Naomi leaves Bethlehem because of a famine, but when she returns she comes back to a harvest. The shift does not signify just a change of season physically, but also spiritually. Perhaps Naomi and her husband did not leave just because of a physical famine, but what if there was a spiritual famine? A spiritual famine is whenever you feel as if God is not speaking and it's hard to understand what God is doing. This is what happens when it seems as if you are living without purpose. God shows Naomi that her purpose resided in a place away from where she thought. God sends us away from comfort to go and find our purpose. Joseph is sent away because his purpose resided in Egypt. Rebekah is sent away to be the queen of many nations. David is sent away because he had to go defeat Goliath and get the kingdom God had planned for him. God sends you away from things on purpose. You may be sent away from certain relationships, jobs, and other perceived opportunities because God has something bigger in store.

The Unexpected Reward

Whenever they arrive in Bethlehem, Naomi tells Ruth to go to the field to pick from the harvest. Naomi challenges Ruth. Think about it. Ruth is unaware of her surroundings (remember she is not from Bethlehem). Naomi still tells her to go. Naomi's response shows us that designated deliverers must be willing to challenge the people they are leading. Ruth obeys and goes to the field to pick from the harvest. Whenever Ruth is gathering the harvest, she meets the owner of the field, Boaz. Boaz gives Ruth enough roasted grain to take home for leftovers. I'd imagine Naomi was amazed with all of the grain Ruth brought back. So, we can see that Naomi benefited from Ruth's obedience. The same source that was feeding Ruth fed Naomi as well. God doesn't just intend to feed the people you are helping, but He wants to feed you as well. The problem with our generation is that we are so caught up in receiving individual rewards, that we sometimes miss God trying to feed us through others.

In Ruth 4, we see that roasted grain isn't the only thing that God intends to provide for designated deliverers. We see throughout the entire book that Naomi challenges Ruth. She tells her to go to the field and to meet with Boaz. She even conspires to get Ruth and Boaz acquainted on the threshing floor. The plan works out

---

A spiritual famine is whenever you feel as if God is not speaking and it's hard to understand what God is doing.

---

for Ruth and Boaz and they get married. However, the marriage is beneficial for Naomi as well. The Lord allowed Ruth to conceive and she gave birth to a son. However, look at what happens. The women living in the town gather around Naomi and say, "Naomi has a son" (Ruth 4:17). Wait? Naomi has a son? This is one of the benefits of a designated deliverer. God gave Naomi a blessing through Ruth. She loses her son in Moab and yet gains a son in Bethlehem. God restores the things she loses through the person that she helps deliver.

Being a designated deliverer is not popular. Oftentimes it is easy to enjoy life by being drunk through worldly temptations. It is hard being a designated deliverer because it requires you to be spiritually coherent while the world is pointing in the opposite direction. The world today is drunk! It is hard to try and point people to Christ, while the world points away from Him. People that have been intoxicated with social media and culture. More importantly, there is a hungry generation. People who are desperately looking for purpose and direction in life. God needs designated deliverers for this world. Through helping others find their purpose, God will allow you to give birth to things that you most likely never even expected. Helping others activate their purpose will allow God to activate the purpose within you.

Designated deliverers help others find their purpose. Finding purpose means that you work to help deliver others from issues so they can find their purpose. Deliverance starts with repentance. Once you know where you are wrong, you begin to focus on what is right! Sometimes this task can be hard because people are so entrenched with the world. It requires you to be patient with people. Before you give up on people, remember how patient God was with you! There are many ways that you can be the designated deliverer. I believe that everyone is a designated deliverer for someone in their life. The problem is...who? If this is your question after reading this chapter, then it is completely okay. As I stated in the beginning of the chapter, being the designated deliverer spiritually is synonymous to being a designated driver naturally. Through the lens of a designated driver, I have outlined three ways that you can learn how to be the designated deliverer for whoever God has assigned for you.

Three Ways to be a Designated Deliverer

1. Obtain Your License

One of the most popular rideshare services today is UBER. The app is full of people that serve as designated drivers across the world. The drivers are of different backgrounds, races, and genders. However, one of the first requirements that UBER presents to its potential drivers is that you must have a valid driver's license. Uber understands the importance of a license because without it the company could be held liable. The license is verification that you can drive and you can be trusted to take their customers to their respective locations. What if I told you that the same thing is true in the spiritual realm?

A lot of people are trying to carry passengers in the spirit without a license. Instead of being licensed by the DMV, in order to be a designated deliverer, you must be licensed by God. I believe that everyone may obtain their license, but everyone's test will look different. Some tests may take longer than others. God wants to know your heart before you lead His people. When I thought about get-

---

Being a designated deliverer is all about helping others to find their purpose.

---

ting my driver's license, there was a book that I was given in order to study. I was already familiar with driving with my permit, so I thought that I didn't have to study. However, my dad told me, *"You better study because you're only taking it once."* In my mind, I was frightened. I was thinking to myself, *"If I don't get it this time, I will never have my license."* So, I began to study more and what I realized was that there was a lot that I didn't know! Obtaining your spiritual license requires you to read the Bible! The Bible will teach you how to lead people and help you to pass your test to be a deliverer for God's people.

Your license is not just dependent on studying the Bible but also studying people. Jesus' entire ministry was centered on His ability to connect with people. Some of the best UBER drivers that I have dealt with were great because they understood it was more than the ride, it was about the experience. Being a leader and God's designated deliverer requires learning how to connect with people. Do you think Moses would have been able to lead thousands of people if he didn't connect with them? The good thing is that God is our driving instructor. He teaches us the way to obtain a license to be a designated deliverer for Him. It is our choice whether we will learn from Him in order to lead the flock He has picked for us.

2. Find Your Area

When I think about Naomi, in order to find the person she was assigned to carry into purpose, she first had to know where to find her. The "where" in life is just as important as the "who" and the "why." God has shown through many people that, in life, location matters. Whether it be through Abraham, Moses, or David each of them has to relocate in order to carry God's people into their designed purpose. You have to be aware of where God is telling you to go. Then, you will not only find the people that God has created for you to help, but you will also know where to take them.

Understand, when I say your area, it is not just a certain physical location that God may be calling you to serve people. It also relates to your specific anointing. What areas in your life do you consider yourself to be an expert? Take some time to think about this one. What are some gifts that you were born with? These gifts are not only meant to help you but are also meant to help others find their purpose. Take some time to pass on your expertise to others, so that they can begin to grow as well.

The best way that I can explain this is with farming. God places people in our life to serve as soil while we grow. We are the plant, God provides the living water, but we must be in the right environment to grow. The soil represents our environment, this can be your social circle, job, or your location. What is your soil? Does your soil supply you with the necessary nutrients to grow? If yes, great! If not, then you may need to rearrange things in your life that may be hindering your growth. Conversely, you must acknowledge the people around you and make sure that you are being "good soil" for them to grow. Check the soil that you have and the soil that you are giving. Your soil determines your growth, find good soil!

3. Find Your People

The key to being a great leader is to be led by the right person. Being led by the wrong person can have adverse effects on your own leadership. The first question that you should ask yourself when spotting a leader is who is leading them? Doing this will help you understand some of the qualities that the leader will possess. You must find the right leader for you! It might not be in your family or in your church, but the right leader is waiting to lead you. The right leader in your life will encourage, strengthen, and cover you through seasons of your life. Be careful! The change in your season may call for a change in your leader. Sometimes you can outgrow your leader! It is not their fault; they were only necessary for a specific season of your life. In each season of your life, start by evaluating yourself, then you will understand the leadership that you need.

I know this may sound shocking to you, but a lot more people look up to you than you can imagine. Oftentimes, we are so busy looking up to others that we don't realize the number of people looking up to us. It is important that you realize God has called you to lead. Being a designated deliverer is not just about finding people to lead, but also finding the RIGHT people to lead. You have the gifts and all the talent in the world, but if you aren't leading the right people then your effectiveness will be limited. The reason why it feels at times that "no one understands you" may not be your leadership, but simply just the people you are leading.

* * *

What's the Big Idea?

Jesus Himself was a designated deliverer. Like Moses, He was called down from a high place and was assigned to deliver a generation. Instead of Moses' physical mountain, Jesus' "mountain" was the right hand of the throne. He was called down to Earth to deliver people from the traps of religious zealots and save them from the dangers of sin. Before Jesus arrived, the Israelites endured 400 hundred years of silence. Many religious leaders used the Law from

> **The change in your season may call for a change in your leader.**

the Torah (Genesis-Deuteronomy) to guide their lives during this period. They were not wrong with this approach. Since they could not hear directly from God, the Torah was the only guide they could follow to understand how to live.

What happened was that they became more focused on the mechanics of religion, that they neglected the relationship with Christ. It is evident when Jesus is amongst the Pharisees, and they don't even recognize that the Messiah has come. I have always asked myself, how can the Pharisees be so knowledgeable about the Word of God and completely miss the Messiah right in front of them? God shows us through the life of Jesus that sometimes we can get "drunk" with religion. We get caught up in church traditions and rituals that it can cause us to miss Jesus. There are people in the church today that have a better relationship with their pastor than with Jesus. Why? The Bible is misinterpreted. Throughout history, leaders have constantly manipulated God's word just to appease an audience.

The misinterpretation of the Law caused people to miss Jesus. The Law was meant to serve as a guide, but people were guided the wrong way. Therefore, God sends Jesus to fix bad theology. Jesus meets all of the qualifications of a designated deliverer. His life embodies every characteristic of a designated deliverer. Jesus starts by obtaining His license. Jesus waits 30 years to begin His public ministry. Three entire decades before Jesus can go out into the world. You may not have to wait 30 years regarding your life, but do not try and rush God's promises for your life. Timing is everything. God is not only preparing you for the "what" and the "why," but also the "when." Jesus' ministry was so effective because He waits until the right time. So, don't be discouraged when God makes you wait. Just tell yourself, *"My time is coming!"*

Once it was time for Jesus to begin ministering throughout the world, He goes to John the Baptist. Even though Jesus was God, He still submits to John the Baptist.

Don't miss this!

Jesus does not only humble Himself with His time but He was also willing to serve under another leader. Think about it. Jesus, the Messiah, chooses to serve under the man that is preparing the way for Him. That would be difficult for anyone. Jesus humbled Himself even more through another one of His actions. Jesus, who knew no sin, still chooses to get baptized. So, Jesus submits not only to the leader but also to the leader's established process of water baptism. Jesus shows us that humbleness is the key to effectiveness. If He would've come into the wilderness attempting to change everything, John's disciples would have been less inclined to follow Him. To obtain our license as a designated deliverer, we must be humble. Like Jesus, we must take the time to learn the people and the process. To be the change, we must know what to change.

After Jesus gets baptized, the heavens open, and God says, "This is my Son, whom I love; with him, I am well pleased" (Matthew 3:17). Talk about an endorsement! Jesus' ministry is validated from that one comment alone. Similar to Jesus, the same thing occurs when we are reborn in Christ. We don't have to spend our entire lives trying to please God. Everything in your life is validated once you are reborn.

The Spirit falls on Jesus as He comes out of the water. Look at what the Spirit does after it rests on Him. The Spirit leads Jesus into the wilderness to be tempted by the devil (Matthew 4). Jesus spends forty days being tested by the enemy. Jesus understood that before

To be the change, we must know what to change.

He could minister to people, He had to be willing to be tested. He went to obtain His license. You can't get your driver's license without going through a test. If you haven't taken a driving test, no one will trust you to drive a car. The same is true for being a designated deliverer. Jesus was able to effectively minister to people because He was faced with the same temptation. There are times where God puts us through situations not to hurt us, but to test us. The tests in your testimony will give you the ability to minister to more people.

As Jesus begins to preach, His next step is to find the right area. After receiving news that John the Baptist was put in prison, Jesus goes to Galilee. During this time, Galilee was a highly-populated area filled with hungry souls. John's departure from the northern part of Palestine meant that there was an opportunity for Jesus to preach the Gospel to more people. Jesus understood that He needed to reach more people, and it required Him to go to the right location. Are you in the right location? Galilee is not just about your physical area; it is about the opportunity. Jesus could have easily stayed where He was and continued to preach. However, He realized that to be the most effective, He had to take His "Galilee opportunity." What's your Galilee opportunity? It can represent a multitude of things in your life. A business opportunity, career path, college decision, or even a relationship. What opportunity has presented itself in your life that you are questioning? Your apprehension could be the very thing holding you back from your purpose.

After Jesus arrives in Galilee, He chooses to reside in Capernaum. So we see that Jesus chooses the right area WITHIN the right area. Capernaum for Jesus was not only a great location to minister, but it was also the fulfillment of prophecy: "Land of Zebulun and land of Naphtali, the Way of the Sea, beyond the Jordan, Galilee of the Gentiles - the people living in darkness have seen a great light; on those living in the land of the shadow a light has dawned" (Isaiah 9:1-2).

Understand, your assigned area is prophetic! It is no coincidence that you like a specific area or have dreams about a particular place. It is all prophetic! God has that special area assigned for you. It is up to you to get prepared and go where God is calling for you to be. You can see Jesus' area was prophetic because of the impact that He has while residing there. Look at all the miracles that Jesus performed in Capernaum. He heals a demon-possessed man (Mark 1:21), heals a royal official's son (John 4:46), and even heals a centurion's servant by just speaking (Matthew 8:8). Even though Jesus has the power to heal from anywhere, I believe that He shows us that getting into the right location is important. The right location will allow you to contact the right people to use your skills and abilities effectively. Before you chase the people, you have to make sure you get in the right area. God has a special place for you! Once you find it, God will amaze you with the amount of impact you will have.

Jesus realizes one important thing while planning His ministry...He couldn't do it alone. Jesus understood the importance of a team. Note this. If Jesus couldn't do His work alone, then neither can you! Too often in life, we are determined to reach our goals by ourselves. One of the urban colloquialisms that we have adopted today is, "*It is lonely at the top.*" For good leaders, the top is never lonely. Jesus realized that transforming the world wasn't just about performing miracles but also developing leaders. I would change that statement and say, "*When you are a good leader, the top should be crowded with all the people you have uplifted.*" Think about it. The disciples that Jesus teaches go on to start the church. Finding the right

Your assigned area is prophetic!

people is not only crucial for your organization now, but it also affects your legacy.

Let's look at how Jesus finds the right people for His ministry. The first example is with His initial disciples, Simon, and Andrew. Jesus is standing by the lake and sees two struggling fishermen washing their nets. The washing of their nets meant that their fishing day was over with another day of disappointment. Jesus steps into the boat with the men and instructs them to cast their nets out again. Since Jesus was now in the boat, the result would look much different! Once they pulled up the nets from the water, there were so many fish that the boat began to tip over. The men instantly embrace Jesus as Lord and leave everything to follow Him.

There are three things that Jesus does that teach us to find the right people and convince them:

1. Get in the Boat

The first thing that we see Jesus do is He gets in the boat with the disciples. As a designated deliverer, we must get in the boat with our people. See, Jesus wasn't just getting into a physical boat; he was stepping into their spiritual boat. He understands their disappointment from not being able to catch anything. A lot of times, we try to lead people that we don't understand. You must learn about people's situations because it will help you know how to lead them. Getting on the boat requires vulnerability. Authenticity requires vulnerability. People will be open with you only if you are open with them. In order to do this, you must get over the trauma of your past. Oftentimes, it is hard to deal with things in your past. It is necessary that you confront this trauma, because wrestling with your old self is what will make your ministry even more powerful. Not only will you be able to relate to people because you went through something similar, but you can also encourage them by overcoming it!

Another essential thing to note from Jesus is His confidence. Simon complains to Jesus when He instructs the men to cast their nets again, "Master, we've worked hard all night and haven't caught anything. But because you say so, I will let down the nets" (Luke 5:5). The men had the confidence to let down their nets again because their leader had confidence. Understand, people can sense doubt from a mile away! It is necessary to get in the boat with people and have faith that you can help them change their situation.

2. Be a Servant Leader

Jesus knew that Simon and Andrew would be His disciples. However, He doesn't approach them with demands, nor does He even tell them who He truly is. Too often, we overemphasize titles. Jesus shows us that labels don't matter because people will understand your title through your actions. Simon later tells Jesus, "You are the Messiah, the Son of the living God" (Matthew 16:16). Jesus never had to boast about Himself; neither should you. Once people see your value, then they will give you an appropriate title. Before Jesus offers them the opportunity to become disciples, He helps with their issues. In John Maxwell's *21 Irrefutable Laws of Leadership*, one of the laws he outlines is the "law of connection." Maxwell states, "Effective leaders know that you first have to touch people's hearts before you ask them for a hand."

Jesus exemplifies this principle on the boat with the men. The problem in our lives is that we often get this principle confused. Today, we ask for people's hands first and then try to touch their hearts. Is this you? Whenever you deal with people, your mindset should always be "how can I help you?" Doing this will allow people to recognize your value, then they will be more willing to help contribute to your goals and aspirations. Just like a designated driver, they serve people first then receive a reward. The same is true for designated deliverers. To be effective as a leader, you must serve first!

3. Cast The Vision

Jesus shows His value by exceeding the men's expectations with the number of fish they bring into the boat. Jesus steps into the boat to help the men, and THEN He informs the men of His vision. The important thing to note is that the vision should come last whenever you build a team. Often, we prioritize these steps incorrectly and cast the vision first. Understanding the men's situation allowed Jesus to know how He can convey the message so that they could adequately interpret His vision. "Come, follow me," Jesus said, "and I will send you out to fish for people" (Matthew 4:19).

Jesus recognizes that He is dealing with fishermen. To properly communicate the vision, He uses a fishing metaphor to show the impact that the disciples could have. In the same way, as leaders, understanding people allows us to communicate our vision effectively. If people are going to follow you, they must understand WHY they are following you. Even God uses "milk and honey" to describe the Promised Land for the Israelites. He had to use tangible things for the people that would follow Him to remain engaged. God gives designated deliverers the vision for the people that they are called to lead. Our responsibility is to cast that vision effectively so that those that are called to follow can see the vision for themselves.

As designated deliverers, Jesus is our example! Through Jesus, we can see how to lead people effectively. The impact that we will have starts with our ability to connect with those we are called to lead. Nobody wants a selfish leader. People respond to selfless lead-

> "Effective leaders know that you first have to touch people's hearts before you ask them for a hand." -John Maxwell

ers! Our purpose is activated whenever we learn how to deal with people.

Pay close attention!

Everything revolves around people. You may be delivering people, and some people may deliver you. In any case, deliverers are leaders. If you don't feel like God is calling you to deliver anyone in this moment, then this might be your season to prepare. All leaders must grow their leadership skills. God may be putting you through the season of tests to obtain your license. Do not be discouraged with this season! The preparation season is the most necessary season as a designated deliverer. You cannot wait until it's time to lead to say, *"How do I lead?"* No, prepare now! Like Jesus, God honors preparation and will meet your work with His plan. However, if you believe that God is calling you to lead right now, then remember to find your area and find your people. Once you do this, you will reap the benefits by being the most effective leader you can be.

Look at the life of Moses. He spends most of his life in the palace with Pharaoh. His time in the palace allowed him to build relationships and understand the ins and outs of royalty. Fast forward to when God speaks to him in isolation on the mountain. God tells him to lead the Israelites to freedom. For Moses, this is a difficult assignment. He had not previously built the same relationships with enslaved Israelites as he had with the Egyptians. How was he going to lead same Israelites that drove him away? It would have been much easier leading the Egyptians. Whenever Moses goes to plead with Pharaoh about freeing the Israelites, emotions had to be running high. Speaking with Pharaoh wasn't just about him returning to the palace, but it was Moses returning to his old lifestyle. He probably saw people he grew up with along with people speaking a language that he had once spoken.

There was probably a part of Moses that wanted to deliver the Egyptians from the ensuing plagues that would come. However, Moses was self-aware and understood his assignment. Just like Moses, we must have restraint from leading the people we want to lead and focus on those who God has called us to lead. Leading the wrong people causes us to waste our time, energy, and resources on people that don't value them the same as you. Moses would have wasted his time trying to focus on helping the Egyptians because they wouldn't understand him. Yes, this also means that you may not be called to lead those you grew up with! If Moses would have tried to lead the Egyptians, he would have been easily influenced because of his close relationships with them. This is why God had a specific people set out for Moses and in the same way, He has set aside a people for you.

We see this concept applied every election year. Many presidential candidates strategically mark the places around the country where they plan to campaign. The plan for the target areas is based on the political party as well as the candidate's agenda. Political candidates are aware that their leadership is more effective in certain places. Your hometown attracts certain political candidates every year. Why? They know that people will value their message and be more inclined to follow. In the same way, designated deliverers must strategically plan in order to understand the people that God has called them to lead. Pray about the people that He has called you to lead, and He will begin to reveal to you how to find them.

Being a designated deliverer is not difficult, but it does require work. God has given you special gifts in order to activate your purpose, but also to help others activate their purpose. That is what it means to be a designated deliverer. Your ability to help others find their purpose will allow you to see the purpose that God has for you. Remember this! The women rejoiced after Ruth gave birth and exclaimed, "Naomi has a son!" This should be your encouragement that God will allow you to give birth to things if you are committed to serving faithfully to be His designated deliverer.

Thought: Finding your purpose becomes easy whenever you help others to find theirs.

4

Quarantined Purpose

COVID-19 shifted the entire global landscape. For many, the impact of the virus is something we have never seen before. The virus has shifted almost every aspect of our daily lives. Weddings, funerals, and birthdays have all changed! Companies set aside their multi-million-dollar projects to focus on finding a vaccine for this deadly disease. The "new normal" now consists of making sure that you have your wallet, keys, and a mask before leaving your house. Not only has it been difficult adjusting to the "new normal" outside of your home, but there have also been changes to life inside your house. Office chairs have been replaced with recliners. Lunches have gone from a sandwich in the break room with your coworkers to the newest recipe with your family.

The one word to describe this new normal is "quarantine." Why? People around the world have been stuck in their homes every day. Even though the quarantine has hindered people's ability to enjoy their daily activities, God still has used the virus to serve His purpose. There is a renewed energy with many families around the world because of a rise in quality time. Family dinners, game nights, and walks in the neighborhood have occurred more frequently because of the quarantine. More importantly, the quarantine has forced you to focus on yourself. Before the quarantine, there were many different distractions. Our jobs, social media accounts, and relationships have caused us to worry about everyone else, but the virus has limited these distractions.

The quarantine was designed for us to reconnect with God. I believe that the more we have "been on the go," the more we have moved away from God. There are many times where God has allowed things to happen to us to realign our focus. Look at how God treats the Egyptians. He sends plagues for Pharaoh to shift his focus and free the Israelites. Despite Pharaoh's stubbornness, God ultimately got His way. Today, we must focus on God instead of the virus! When you focus on God, you will eliminate distractions and begin to walk on the path He has set for you.

What if I told you that quarantining is necessary? Not just for COVID, but for the rest of your life. I know this might sound crazy. Why should I quarantine if there is no virus? It's what gets you closer to Him. God is showing us during the virus how to quarantine. The valuable things we have learned during the quarantine have improved our efficiency and productivity. The quarantine is how many of us learned to connect with God. Why should we change that? There are lessons learned from this quarantine that we should continue to maintain for the rest of our lives.

There are people in the Bible that quarantine. In the wilderness, Moses constantly quarantines on the mountain to get closer to God. Moses' quarantine didn't consist of Netflix and ice cream. As a leader, Moses realizes that his alone time with God was necessary. Moses was able to hear clearly from God. Think about it. During Moses' alone time, God gave Moses the Ten Commandments. What could God bless you with during your quarantine? There is a purpose whenever God puts us in quarantine. When God places us in quarantine, it allows us to find our purpose. Another prophet who found purpose in quarantine is Jonah. Let's probe into the story of Jonah and get another perspective on the notion of quarantine.

I'M STUCK

God calls Jonah. God gives Jonah an assignment to preach and encourage the Ninevites to repent. At the time, Nineveh was a great city with a grand army. God calls Jonah to go by himself to tell the Ninevites to repent of their sins. What does Jonah do? He runs. Before you judge, there are many times we've run from something God told us to do. When have you run from God? Running in this instance is not just a physical exercise. There have been times that God has forced us to step outside of our comfort zones and we get apprehensive with what He has called us to do. When this happens, we are "running." Jonah sails to Tarshish, and nothing goes as planned. While sailing to Tarshish, a terrible storm endangers Jonah and the rest of the sailors. The storm that occurs in Jonah's life is symbolic of the times in our life when it feels like nothing is going right. The lesson we can learn from Jonah is that running from God can endanger both you and the people connected to you.

To rid the storm, the crew throws Jonah off the boat. Once Jonah is sinking in the water, or better yet in his guilt and shame, God provides a lifeline. You know the story. God sends a large fish to "swallow up" Jonah (Jonah 1:17). Jonah was now stuck in the belly of the fish. So, in a sense, God forces Jonah to quarantine. Jonah put himself in that situation, just like we often do. Maybe we have run to that relationship or job that we knew wasn't any good for us. It felt good at first, but now you feel stuck. It might not be physically, but mentally you feel like Jonah in the fish. I know there had to be times where Jonah asked God, *"what now?"* This stuck place is usually where you get depressed. However, these are the moments that are opportunities to seek God more.

The fish represents whatever you feel is swallowing you in life. What's got you stuck in this season? Is it your bills, relationship, or maybe it might be your family? Sometimes, these simple things can make us feel as if there is no way out. There is a way out! Understand that whenever you feel stuck, God is trying to realign your focus on Him. The season of being "stuck" is between what YOU want to do versus what GOD wants you to do. The Israelites felt stuck in the wilderness. They were stuck because they spent forty years trying to do things their way. Once they began to do things God's way, then God led them to the Promised Land. Are you doing what you want or what God wants? Maybe YOU are the reason that you are being held back from God's promises for your life. Wherever you might be, God can still make a way! Jonah felt stuck while he was quarantined in the fish. In the fish, Jonah gives us critical lessons about handling ourselves whenever we are quarantined.

He Prays

The first chapter is all about what Jonah does to get himself stuck in the belly of the fish. However, look at how chapter two starts, "Then Jonah prayed unto the LORD his God out of the fish's belly" (Jonah 2:1). So, the first thing that Jonah does when he gets stuck is he prays to God. Most of the time, whenever we get stuck, we try to fix things ourselves. We look for people to help us to improve our situation instead of God. When this happens, much like masking ourselves from a virus, we put our "mask on" around God. The mask is holding you back from being vulnerable with God. The mask is intended for people, not for God! Our time in quarantine is meant to connect with God.

The season of being "stuck" is between what YOU want to do
versus what GOD wants you to do.

God wants you to be vulnerable with Him whenever you are
stuck. Whenever you are stuck, He wants you to know that He is
the way out! Look at how vulnerable Jonah is in his prayer. Jonah
says, "I am cast out of thy sight, yet I will look again toward thy holy
temple" (Jonah 2:4). Jonah feels like God has left him. We have all
felt exactly like Jonah. There are times we feel like, "God, where are
you?" Oftentimes, we are afraid to be that vulnerable in our prayers.

Growing up, I thought being that vulnerable with my parents
was a golden ticket to some sort of punishment. Holding my anger
only created more issues because I was afraid to address my concerns truly. However, once I began to express my concerns to my
parents, everything began to change. I started feeling better because
everything that I was holding in was released. The same thing happens spiritually. God is "Abba" which means Father! He protects us
just like any parent should. Whenever we are faced with turmoil in
life, God wants us to call on Him. See, the enemy wants you to hold
your issues from God. Holding things from God only creates more
anger and eventually causes you to act out of character. Newsflash,
that's exactly what the enemy wants! Jonah goes on to say, "yet I will
look again towards thy holy temple." Even though Jonah is stuck, he
chooses to look past his current circumstances and focuses on God.

He Remembers

There's a lot to dissect in Jonah chapter 2. In the previous section, we see that Jonah initially responds to his quarantine by praying. As a result, his prayers cause him to remember God even amid
adversity. Jonah says, "When my life was ebbing away, I remem-

bered you, Lord,' (Jonah 2:7). We see here that one of the benefits of quarantine is reflection. During the pandemic, quarantining has given us the ability to reflect on how good God has been. Many of us can sit with our families in a lovely home and work remotely. Read that sentence again and look at all the things that God has provided. *Family. Home. Job.* Blessings after blessings that show God's faithfulness.

Often, we can get so caught up in the day-to-day activities that we forget God. There are many different distractions that we may face daily. Things like grinding at work, taking care of your kids, and finishing schoolwork could cause you to turn your attention away from God. The only time that we truly rely on God is whenever we face issues. When this happens, we treat God like a genie! So, God had to put the world on halt so that we can understand He is not here just to grant people's wishes.

The quarantine has produced this lethargic feeling for people all over the world. People's plans have gone astray. There has been a sudden shift from celebration to trepidation. We have gone from believing God to questioning Him. Let me ask you this. What if one of the reasons that God has placed us in quarantine is to reflect? I know what you're thinking. What does reflection have to do with my purpose? It has everything to do with it! Anytime we see a breakthrough in the Bible, the next response is always reflection. Even going back to Genesis, whenever Noah gets out of the ark his next action was to build an altar. Once again, reflection.

God has put us in quarantine to remember all the things that He has done for us. Seeing what God has done in our past will prepare us for what He has planned for our future. During your quarantine, remember the promises that God has made for you. God promises to "never leave nor forsake us" (Deuteronomy 31:6). God has not left you! Whenever you may feel stuck, He is right there with you.

Also, remember that God's word doesn't "return to Him void" (Isaiah 55:11). If God promised you something before the pandemic, then it will still come to pass! Don't give up on your assignment. Just because you can't see it, doesn't mean nothing is happening! There is power in your patience. As James puts it, "But let patience have its perfect work, that you may be perfect and complete, lacking nothing." (James 1:4). The enemy's desire is for you to give up on God during the quarantine. That voice in your head is probably saying, "*Your business can't stay afloat,*" or better yet, "*That marriage won't last.*" During these moments, don't give up. Remember all the good that God has done! God has remembered you during the quarantine, now it is time you remember Him!

Activation requires reflection. Through reflection, you can better plan your future. One of my former teachers used to phrase it this way, "*You can't know where you're headed if you don't know where you have been.*" God has positioned you for greatness! When you understand how far you've come, you get a glimpse of all the greatness you've already accomplished. You can't quit now! You have come too far to quit. In the difficult moments of life, it is often hard not to focus on anything but your current issue. The key to overcoming any battle in your life is to remember God. Whenever you remember God, you will remember all of those challenging moments that He has already brought you through. Then, you will find comfort in the power of God to fix your situation. In other words, the more time you focus on the goodness of God, the less time you dwell on the problems that the enemy has presented.

He Praises

There are three things Jonah does in his "quarantine." We have already gone over the first two. First, he prays to God. Jonah realizes that his own actions got him stuck in the belly of the fish. Jonah

The more time you focus on the goodness of God, the less time you dwell on the problems that the enemy has presented.

responds to his current situation by turning back to God in prayer. Then, his prayers help him focus more on God. The final part of Jonah's quarantine was his praise.

Jonah begins to praise God while inside the fish. He doesn't let his circumstance dictate his praise. For some of us, a simple stain on your clothes is enough to stop our praise! Adversity in our lives usually causes us to spit out some "not so nice words." You know this is true! Jonah's praise should be an example for us. That no matter what happens, we should always continue to praise God!

Often, we think that praise and worship is meant only for early Sunday mornings. Praise is not limited to a specific day, time, or location! Praise also isn't limited to just singing gospel! You can praise him through dancing or just simply saying, *"Thank you, Lord!"* You don't need an audience to praise God. Look at where Jonah praises God! He praises God from inside of a fish! If God can hear someone from the belly of a fish, He can hear you from anywhere! You can praise God wherever you are! Your praise is not limited to a physical church building. You are the church! Let your praises be heard from the living room, your desk, even the bathroom. Yes, God can hear you even in your bathroom! Understand this. God is wherever your praise is. God wants your praises even when you are stuck in life like Jonah.

To understand the importance of Jonah's praise, we must dive deeper into what he says to God. Jonah says, "But I, with shouts of grateful praise, will sacrifice to you. What I have vowed I will make good. I will say, 'Salvation comes from the LORD." There is a lot that you can pull from in Jonah's statement to God. The most salient point is when he asserts, "What I have vowed I will make good" (Jonah 2:9). Jonah makes a bold declaration to God that things would turn around for him. I believe that God was waiting for this declaration from Jonah. God wanted Jonah to know for himself that he had the power to change his situation.

God has many names, but the name that speaks to the heart of God is Heavenly Father. Whenever we think of God as our father, we can see similarities between God and our earthly parents. There comes a moment in every child's life that parents let their children make decisions for themselves. I have heard it referred to as *"taking the training wheels off."* God does the same thing with us, spiritually. In the infant stage, God will direct every step for us. As we grow in Christ, God gives us more responsibility and trusts us with our decisions. When we got into trouble as a kid running to our parents was necessary, but we had to figure things out ourselves as we grew older. Our parents force us to learn things ourselves because it builds our problem-solving and critical thinking skills.

If you grew up without a parent, no worries! Think about your life as a student. God is also our instructor. David writes in Psalms 32:8, "I will instruct you and teach you in the way which you should go; I will counsel you with My eye upon you." A good instructor doesn't give all the answers to the students. As our instructor, God uses tough moments to enhance our executive agency and improve our ability to reason. If you ever feel like you're going through a test like Jonah, God is probably preparing you for graduation into your next season.

God puts us through trials in life for us to understand that He has created us to be the answer. God has given us everything that we need to get unstuck! It is up to us to believe it. Your season between being stuck and where God wants you to be starts with you! Like Jonah, it is time to start talking yourself out of being stuck. You can talk yourself out of that depression and anxiety. Things will change, but it starts with you!

Transport to Purpose

Jonah's prayers lead to his reflection, and all that results in him praising the Lord. The result of all of Jonah's actions leads to one thing, freedom. God commands the fish to spit Jonah out. When the fish spits out Jonah, he appears on dry land. Different from the point where Jonah initially starts, God takes him to a new place. Symbolically, the dry land represents a new beginning. Even in Exodus, when Moses and the Israelites passed through the Red Sea, they passed through on dry land (Exodus 14:21). God wants you to come out of your quarantine into dry land! Paul writes, "The past has been forgotten, and our spirits have been renewed" (1 Corinthians 5:7). When we give our troubles to God, He gives us a new beginning! God wanted Jonah to focus on the task in front of him more than his past. He wants the same thing for us. Jesus Christ has given us a chance at a new beginning. We have been renewed and restored. Dwelling in the past can potentially make us stuck again! God wants to show you that any traces of your past have been washed away. It is time for you to step onto the dry land and into your destiny!

What intrigues me so much about how God deals with Jonah is that He still fulfilled His intended purpose. God can even use a fish to carry purpose! Initially, Jonah probably thought that he had nowhere to go and that his life was nearing death. God had other plans for Jonah's life! Despite Jonah's rebellion, God still chose him. Even though Jonah thought he was stuck in the fish, God used the fish to carry Jonah to a new beginning. In other words, God used the fish to transport Jonah to fulfill His purpose. God is doing the same for you! What is the thing in your life that you feel has swallowed you whole and has made you stuck? Is it your finances?

Maybe, your classes. Whatever "it" is that makes you feel stuck is the very thing that God is using to take you to a new beginning.

In college, I suffered from depression. I was stuck. I believed that I had nowhere to turn. Everything on the outside seemed to be perfect. I was in a relationship and just crossed into a fraternity. Socially and emotionally, I was at an all-time high, but mentally I was a train wreck. As a result, I constantly had suicidal thoughts. I felt that life lost its meaning. In the face of adversity, I turned to God. The transition spiritually allowed me to build my foundation with God. From there, everything began to change for me. My prayer life changed. I attended church more frequently and became friends with more believers in Christ. As I grow spiritually, God has shown me that I have a calling for ministry. Even though I believe that God would have eventually shown me that He wanted this path for my life, ironically, depression catalyzed me finding my calling.

In the same way, God used what I thought was holding me hostage to transport me to my purpose is the same way He can transport you! You may run away from things, but it is now time to embrace whatever is troubling you. For you, it might not be depression. It might be your job. That job may feel like your "fish," but it could be God carrying you to a new beginning. Don't give up in your "fish." Not only does God send the fish for Jonah so that he wouldn't drown in water, but neither would he drown from his sin and guilt. You feeling stuck is not God punishing you, but it is God transporting you.

Let's look at the life of a butterfly. Many people see butterflies and observe their beauty as they fly. Butterflies are indeed beautiful creatures, but for the beauty to ever develop, they must quarantine. We call it a cocoon, but I would imagine caterpillars see this stage as a quarantine. It has always intrigued me when I see caterpillars crawling along the ground. I think to myself, "Does the caterpillar know that eventually, it will become a butterfly?" The caterpillar forms the cocoon, and changes happen. The quarantine for us should let us know that change is coming as well. We aren't stuck. We are merely changing.

Don't miss this point.

Whenever caterpillars are in quarantine, they must change their bodies and must also change their mindset. Going from a caterpillar to a butterfly is about a mindset shift.

Think about it. If butterflies leave their cocoons still thinking that they are a caterpillar, they will always think they are meant to crawl along the ground. This mindset will only result in the butterfly neglecting its gifts. We mustn't make this same mistake. We cannot exit the quarantine with the same mindset that we entered. God has called you to fly! Your crawling season is over, it is time for you to soar! Butterflies occupy the same space as the caterpillar, but now they have a different worldview. Just like the butterfly, our perspective of the world should change after the quarantine. For this to happen, our minds must evolve!

After Jonah leaves the fish, God gives him the same command as in the beginning. Instead of running like the first time, Jonah quickly accepts God's command. Jonah understands now that his decisions are life and death. Butterflies leaving the cocoon can't decide if they want to fly or not. They must quickly accept their change. In this season, God is preparing us for opportunities that will happen after the quarantine. The reality is that the opportunities presented might look and feel the same before the virus happened. The same opportunities we ran from before, God will allow us to redeem ourselves. The critical thing to remember is that we must operate quickly with these opportunities to receive the fullness of everything God has planned for us.

Many of you are stuck right now, even after reading this chapter. The question every morning in your mind is, *"What do I do about*

Your crawling season is over, it is time for you to soar!

_____?" The blank can be filled with things like a specific class, your marriage, or sickness. There is a struggle to get "unstuck." During these times, it is probably hard to see the benefits of your quarantine. Trust me, there are benefits. We must learn how to find them. Every leader must know these essential tips to make the most out of their quarantine.

To be successful, every leader must make it a routine to quarantine. Again, I am not saying quarantine necessarily because of a virus. Your quarantine can be your quiet time with God. This time allows you to focus on yourself, realign your priorities, and seek God.

Too many opinions can only cloud what God is trying to say. Understand, people are not wrong for their views. Wise counsel is indeed beneficial and necessary. The issue is that people are only giving their limited perspective, but our God knows everything. He knows the beginning and the end. We must emphasize hearing from the source instead of the resource.

Steps to Quarantine Effectively

1. Find Your Place

First, you must find your quarantine location. Establish a place that you want to go to commune with God. Quarantining can happen from your bedroom, the park, or a simple walk through your neighborhood. Somewhere you know that you can seclude yourself from people to focus on God truly. Once you find that place, then make it personal. Maybe you bring a blanket, a pillow, or even a lamp. Making the space unique allows you to be comfortable as you pursue God.

Kids do this all the time. Whenever they build their imaginary forts, they customize the design based on their preferences. After it is completed, no one can come to their fort. It is invitation only. Why? The fort gives them access to a world of imagination. To you, it may look like a couple of chairs put together with a blanket over the top. To them, it's a place that is full of superheroes and scenes from the latest action movie. The same intimacy that kids experience in their quarantine is available to you as well. Everyone doesn't need to know the place where you go to communicate with God! Nor can everyone have access. Moses understood this. God wants to talk to YOU! To hear God, you must focus on Him.

Now, understand, making your space unique doesn't mean filling it with distractions. Your place should focus more on intimacy than intricacy. If worship music helps you to communicate with God, bring your headphones. There are ways to make the place your own without inviting distractions. Look around your house, in your car, and around your city to find that place for you. Find it and try to go daily. The good news is as you look forward to arriving there each day, God is already there waiting for you!

2. Find Your Time

Next, establish when you want to quarantine. Mornings are popular for leaders to start their day. Almost all of the business articles show that CEOs' and high-level executives' success is mainly attributed to their early morning start. Research says that waking up early increases productivity. Think about how much more productive you would be if your mornings started with God. Starting your morning with God allows you to live out Proverbs 3:5-6. You are choosing to trust God at the beginning of your day. When God sees that, then He will guide you through the day. Before bed, you will look back and be amazed at how much you accomplished because you trusted God with your day. How do you do this? Start by waking up an hour earlier so that you can devote that time to God.

Good news! I am not a morning person either. Ha! I know you read that discouraged because you struggle to get up in the morning. You can still have quality time with God! If you are a late riser, then maybe your time could be later in the day. Set aside some time midday to interact with God. If you work, eat your lunch early and use those extra minutes to talk with God. Those don't work either? Then you can enjoy my favorite, winding down with God. I love ending my day reading the Bible and talking to God. The best way to eliminate the stress and anxiety after a long day is to finish the day hearing from God. Setting the times aside at night has multiple benefits. Not only does it give you guidance for issues faced during the day, but it also helps to plan out the day ahead.

The point is that there is no perfect time. Just because you are an early riser or night owl doesn't mean that you are more anointed. Whatever time is best for you then set it aside on your schedule. It's not about the actual time. It's about what you do WITH the time. Keep that time at the forefront of your mind and make sure that you follow your schedule. After a while, it will become second nature and you will not be able to get through your day without your time with God.

3. Be Intentional

Once you find the time and place, the last step is to be intentional with your quarantine. Remember how intentional Jonah was in his prayers to God? We must also be intentional about the things we are looking to accomplish with our time with God. If it's just 30 minutes, take that half an hour seriously. Put away your phone.

Communicate with God and then take time to listen to what He is telling you.

God responds to your boldness. This is one of the reasons why I love the prophet, Elisha. The boldness of Elisha was the reason he received the double portion of Elijah's spirit. He simply speaks up about exactly what he wanted. In the same light, you must be bold with your time with God. You must let God know what you want. Not for Him, but for you. Think about your parents. Whenever the holidays roll around, the common question is, *"What do you want for Christmas?"* You have a choice to tell them what you want. As a kid, my suggestion for gifts would be extraordinary. My response went something like, *"I want four pairs of Jordan's, an XBOX, a new bike, and two Polo shirts."* I was not afraid to tell them exactly what I wanted. However, as I got older, I started to realize that all these gifts cost money. I wanted to be more conservative, so my response changed to, *"Whatever is fine with me."* The reality is we treat God the same way. If you sit down and listen to the prayers of a kid it is very specific with every issue they are currently facing. As we get older, we lose that touch and make all of our prayers to fit a more traditional pattern. God knows exactly what you want, He is simply waiting for you to tell Him.

Wait!

Be careful not to get caught up asking God for things. I had to learn this as well. Whenever you spend your time coming to God for His blessings then we lose touch because we become spiritual gold diggers. Uh oh! Instead of asking for things, change your focus and just ask for God. Be intentional! Tell God that your goal with your prayer is to seek Him. The truth is that once you have God, all of the things you want will work themselves out.

You must be intentional with the time you have. God loves discipline. Discipline doesn't mean that you can't have fun, nor does it mean that you have to do the same thing daily. If you are intentional with the Lord, then He will reveal your purpose. Leaders must be disciplined. Leaders benefit from this because God will give purpose not only for you but also for the people you are leading. Find your place. Find your time. Be Intentional.

* * *

What's the Big Idea?

For three years, we see the impact of Jesus' ministry. Jesus revolutionizes Christianity through His countless miracles and parables. One of the secrets, why Jesus was able to be so effective, was isolation. There are many instances where Jesus goes in solitude to hear from God. Even though He is both man and God, Jesus shows us that isolation was still necessary. I believe that Jesus realized that His fleshly parts suggested things to Him, but His isolation allowed Him to recalibrate and lean into His spirit. In the same way, we are in a constant battle between flesh and spirit. Since we were born into sin, naturally, our flesh tends to focus on ourselves instead of on God. The struggle can be from sexual desires to overeating at the dinner table. Ha! Both can cause significant repercussions! The reason that we fast is so that we can do as Jesus does and humble our flesh to our spirit. As we discussed earlier, isolation is preparation for your purpose. Throughout the life of Jesus, many people interacted with Jesus daily. The consequence of His interaction was that there were many different voices. Even amongst his disciples, they each had their own opinion of the things that Jesus should do. Think about when Jesus passes through the Samaritan village. After the Samaritan rejects Jesus and His disciples, James and John say, "Lord, do you want us to tell fire to come down from heaven and consume them" (Luke 9:54). Jesus had to turn and rebuke them because their feelings were corrupting their thoughts. If Jesus had listened to them in that instance, it would have turned Him away from His purpose. Therefore, Jesus constantly quarantines Himself so that He can hear from His spirit about how to operate.

Similarly, we must be conscious of the voices that we listen to both externally and internally. There will be many people around you who will try to instruct you on how you should live your life. Whenever you listen to others over listening to God, chaos ensues. However, another problem is that others aren't the only ones talking to us, it is also yourself. Think about the last time you had to make a big decision. Did you take time to listen to what God wanted, or was your decision based on what you wanted? The biggest battles we often face are with the conflicting voices in our heads. *Which voice am I supposed to listen to?* Be mindful of the things that you are telling yourself. You must make sure that you consult God about your decisions before you act. David acted based on his thoughts with Bathsheba and look at what resulted! He ends up killing his most loyal servant, and his firstborn dies. Do not risk losing people close to you or killing things you've given birth to because you acted in your own will instead of God's.

Let's go back to Jesus. There is one instance in particular where Jesus quarantines. In Mark 1, Jesus heals many people and drives out demons. After Jesus finishes teaching and performing miracles, look at what he does: "Very early in the morning, while it was still dark, Jesus got up, left the house, and went off to a solitary place, where he prayed. Simon and his companions went to look for him, and when they found him, they exclaimed: "Everyone is looking for you!" Jesus replied, "Let us go somewhere else—to the nearby villages—so I can preach there also. That is why I have come" (Mark 1:38). And so it was...He traveled throughout Galilee, preaching in their synagogues and driving out demons.

Jesus quarantines!

Now that you know how to quarantine, let's learn how to quarantine like Jesus. There are three main takeaways in Jesus' quarantine that I believe will help you be more effective.

1. Quarantine in the Dark

Initially, we see that Jesus wakes up to pray to God. On the surface, we think that this must be part of His daily routine. However, I want to dig deeper and look past the text. I believe that the Bible is not just referring to physical darkness, but spiritual darkness as well. With this logic, Jesus shows us that He quarantines amid chaos. Think about it. In the section before He quarantines, we see that He heals many people. He helps Simon's mother-in-law with her fever, drives out impure spirits, and even cures people of various diseases. What a day! Jesus has a lot of things on His plate, and it could have been very chaotic. Now, because it is Jesus, He can handle it. However, Jesus still quarantines to help us understand what we should do during the chaos.

There will be chaotic times in our lives where it feels as if we have a lot on our plate. Even though there is a new day, your situation still seems dark. During these times, we often try to handle everything ourselves. Whenever you do this, your situation will only get darker. In your adversity, quarantine! Isolating yourself IN chaos allows you to separate yourself FROM chaos. Whenever we isolate to find God, everything is ordered for us. God is a God of order, not chaos. God has the power to order everything that may seem chaotic in your life today! All you have to do is seek Him! If Jesus has to quarantine, then so should you!

To isolate Himself, Jesus leaves the house to go to a solitary place. So, Jesus physically removes Himself to find God. Jesus changes His environment because that is where the chaos originated. If Jesus would have stayed, He probably would have heard other people's voices. Jesus had to remove Himself! The disciples often asked Jesus about prayer because He often removes Himself even from them. Like Jesus, you must remove yourself!

The first step in fixing any issue in your life is to remove yourself from the situation. We must change our environment to get intimate with God. Think about that person in your life. Whenever you are with your significant other, hanging out with each other's friends is cool for a while, but there comes a moment when you want to be alone with each other. Being alone is where you get to be intimate and express your feelings. The same is true with your relationship with God. You must make an effort, like Jesus, to get close to God. You may have to take a moment to get away from your friends and even your family. The people close to you are not wrong for their opinion. What you have to realize is that God's voice is more significant than any other voice.

2. Believe what you Heard

As usual, Jesus is in high demand. While isolating Himself, the disciples go to find Jesus. As soon as the disciples meet him, they tell Him, *"Everyone is looking for you!"* Typically, Jesus would have gone back and spent His time helping everyone that wanted to see Him. However, this time, look at what Jesus says. Jesus replied, "Let us go somewhere else—to the nearby villages—so I can preach there also." Jesus responds differently than He would have previously. I believe that God told Jesus to go elsewhere. Jesus had to be obedient at this moment because it was necessary to expand to more places.

Obedience is the key to success. There are many times where God has asked people to do something different for a specific reason. My mother says it this way, *"Don't go where everybody goes...I didn't raise everybody."* Just because everyone was looking for Jesus did not mean that is where God called him to go. Jesus quarantining

God's voice is more significant than any other voice.

Himself allowed Him to get clarity about His next steps in ministry. Whenever you are quarantined, God may provide an answer that is contrary to what you think is right. Whenever this happens, you must believe what you heard. Believe that whatever God has said is true. There are times when it may not be popular or not the most comfortable option, but you must trust that it is the right option because God said so!

Due to Jesus' obedience, He can continue performing miracles and spread his ministry. While traveling to the nearby villages, He heals a man with leprosy (Mark 1:40) and heals a paralyzed man (Mark 2). It is important in your life not to chase after what is popular, but what is right! Yes, Jesus probably would have still been effective no matter what He did. However, Jesus was able to be more effective in listening to God. Understand, God is strategic and plays the long game! Whenever He performs these miracles in these nearby villages, the people are amazed and spread the news about His power. The widespread news about Jesus was necessary for His purpose. God is not worried about your popularity. He is concerned about your purpose! Therefore, whenever God tells you to do something that you may disagree with, you must be obedient because it is all happening for your good. Believe that you hear from God, and He will begin to push you right into your purpose!

3. Recalibrate your Focus

Quarantining with God not only helps Jesus know where He needs to go; it also helps Him to remember why he must go. After telling the disciples that He must go to the nearby villages, He says, *"That is why I have come."*

Don't miss this!

Jesus realizes a difference between what He was currently doing and what God called him to do. I believe that Jesus remembers this whenever He is praying in a solitary place. Jesus came not to save a couple of people. He came to save the world! To do this, He had to begin to spread His ministry to other places. People in the nearby villages most likely had no clue of Jesus and His power. Due to the importance of His time on Earth, Jesus could not wait for them to understand who He was. Jesus had to go to the people and begin to share the Gospel. Through the towns that He visited, His name and His message have spread throughout the world! Isolating ourselves to seek God will allow us to have the same impact. Worrying about day-to-day activities causes you to lose focus on the bigger picture. God wants to show you the why behind your purpose. Don't get too caught up in the what. Quarantining with God allows you to recalibrate and remember why He has called you!

In middle school, we used what was called a SmartBoard. The SmartBoard revolutionized classrooms across the world. The electronic board allowed for content to come alive by jumping off the screen. Since the SmartBoard automated everything, there would be moments where the board froze or lost its alignment. To fix the issue, all you had to do was recalibrate the board. You pressed the two buttons on the bottom of the board and pressed the dots on the screen to realign the board with the user.

Similarly, quarantining with God allows us to recalibrate so that we can focus on Him. When we focus too much on worldly things, we must recalibrate! You must be aware of when your alignment is off with God. There are many ways that you can tell. When you are struggling in life, what do you do? Do you go to your friends or God? If it is more so the former than the latter, then your alignment is off track. God wants to align you with the purpose He has for your life! For this to happen, you must seek Him so that He can begin to work.

Thought: Every leader must make it a routine to quarantine.

5

Paralyzed Purpose

In the previous chapter, we discussed what happens when you feel stuck in life. In our analysis, we saw through Jonah how to manage your quarantine. Even though we outlined tips and strategies to get the most out of quarantining, what happens when you do everything outlined and still feel stuck? Better yet, what happens when you get too comfortable in your quarantine? I know it sounds preposterous, but the reality is that many people's quarantine IS their new normal. The sad truth is that there will be people who will still be stuck at home because they're faced with fear or confined to their way of life in quarantine.

Outside of the pandemic, we face this issue daily. We get stuck in our ways of life. Everyone is an "addict" of something worldly. It may not be drug-related, but it could be a certain way of life that consumes us. Based on their daily demand, I think most people in the world say they are addicted to Starbucks. Maybe for you it might not be coffee, but social media. The issue with any addiction is that it consumes us. We are so attached to our habits that it feels like we simply can't change.

The truth is that life is all about change. Throughout the Bible, we see change. God changes leaders, environments, and even miracles. Change is the essence of life. The spontaneity of life is what makes it enjoyable. So, if change is something that we enjoy, then, of course, the enemy wants the opportunity to ruin it. How does he accomplish it? One word: cycles. You know what I am talking about! Times where you feel like you have gotten "unstuck" only to fall back into the same traps you did before. Cycles are the enemy's way to make you feel like you are changing, but you end up back in the same place. In Jonathan McReynolds' song, *Cycles*, he says something so profound. He says, *"The enemy learns from your mistakes even if you don't."* This is so true! Cycles have a lasting effect on you because the enemy intends to create bigger traps to keep you from your promise.

After the fall in the garden, the rest of the Old Testament can be summed up in one word, cycles. We see multiple instances where the Israelites are stuck. As a result, they turn to God, and He frees them from bondage. To thank God, the Israelites worship and celebrate. Happily ever after? No. The Israelites turn back to their gods and do their own thing. The Israelites cycles lead them to captivity. Be careful! Cycles only lead to bondage. Are you currently dealing with cycles? Not sure? You are fine! Most of the time, you aren't even aware. What a trick of the enemy! The good news is that God has sent a solution to break your cycles. The solution is Jesus Christ! We can be freed from whatever bondage we may go through because of His blood. While on earth, Jesus broke cycles. He healed a woman with an issue of blood who was going through a twelve-year cycle of rejection; He stepped on a boat with a fisherman who went through a cycle of catching nothing and changing the course of his life. There are many different instances where Jesus breaks other's cycles, and He can break whatever is holding you hostage, as well. Let's take a look specifically at a story where Jesus' power frees a man from bondage.

In Luke 5, Jesus heals a paralyzed man. Groups of Pharisees and teachers of the law all came to see Jesus preach. You would probably imagine people gathering in excitement to see Jesus teach and perform miracles. Wrong! The Pharisees were anxious to see if Jesus would break the law. Despite all the hostility, God gives Jesus the power to heal the people that were gathered. I know you're asking, "Heal them from what?" Only people that are sick need healing. Right? Exactly. Jesus recognizes that people among Him are sick. People in the crowd weren't just sick physically but spiritually as well. Jesus understands the severity of the situation. Many of the people had never witnessed His power. So, their belief in Jesus had only come from the things that they heard.

Is this where you are? Have you ever come to the point where you "kind of" believe in Jesus? Trust me. It's okay to say yes. Later in the chapter, we will discuss more how to deal with that state of mind. Whenever you are low in faith you become spiritually sick. You are unable to believe because you've been met with so many disappointments. The good news is that God gives us a prescription called vision. God positions the crowd for them to see the coming miracle and restore their faith. God restores faith by restoring vision. God shows us His power through others, so that we can understand how He has the power to change our life. How does this relate to you? God could be performing miracles on the people around you so that you can regain your faith and believe that He can do it for you!

When we discuss the paralyzed man's story, I have always heard many different perspectives preached on the topic of healing. Pastors have preached the message about the friends that help bring the paralyzed man to Jesus. Multiple sermons have discussed Jesus' response to the Pharisees while healing the man. However, I have al-

God restores faith by restoring vision.

ways wondered why don't we ever talk about the paralyzed man on the mat? I have many questions about this man and what probably went through his mind when he sees Jesus. Once seeing the story from the paralyzed man's perspective, I began to see similarities to my life. I came to the realization that changed my life forever. I said this to myself, *"I've been paralyzed."*

Paralyzed Purpose

The truth is that we've all been paralyzed. In fact, you could be paralyzed right now. In the King James Version, the man is described as having palsy (Luke 5:18). Today, the word palsy can be associated with the prevalent disorder, Cerebral palsy. This disorder affects our ability to move.

In the same way, many of us have dealt with spiritual disorders in our lives. Whenever we have spiritual disorders, we get stuck in seasons of our life. There are many ways that we can become paralyzed spiritually. The enemy has hit you with blows, and life hits you hard. You begin to think, like the paralyzed man, that you can't get up.

How does this happen? Let's start from the beginning. Since the beginning of time, God has given each of us a unique purpose. In the first chapter, we discussed that many people are living with de-activated purposes. This is the enemy's goal...keep people ignorant of their purpose. There are three ways that the enemy attempts to keep you from purpose: fear, seduction, and lying.

Goliath was chosen by the Philistines to instill fear in the Israelites (1 Samuel 17). The same Philistines use Delilah to seduce Sampson (Judges 16). In the garden, we see that the enemy lies whenever he tells Eve that the fruit will make them like God (Genesis 3:5). These are all forms of the enemy's distractions. All of these are meant to keep us paralyzed spiritually. Let's evaluate the story further. Jesus sees the faith of the man's friends. The friends go to the point of going on top of the roof to get their friend healed. Talk about friends that are "*Ride or Die!*" Jesus heals the paralyzed man. Not in the way that we would imagine. He starts by telling the man, "Friend, your sins are forgiven" (Luke 5:20). Why does Jesus start this way? Jesus shows us that healing must begin from the inside before it can ever manifest on the outside. People are stuck today simply because there has been a false assumption that healing only happens on the outside, but true healing is wholeness. God wants to heal you on the inside. God evaluates your heart then changes things around you. Look at how God changes David's occupation and status because he was a man after His heart. You may feel stuck because God is waiting for things on the inside of you to change.

Jesus has to let the paralyzed man on the mat know that his sins were forgiven because his guilt caused him to be paralyzed. Don't let your guilt hold you down. You know that feeling you get right after you've sinned? Unnecessary weight gets on your shoulders, and you don't feel like doing anything for the rest of the day. Our sin begins to paralyze us because it controls our spiritual muscles, making us incapable of movement.

Let's jump back to the idea of wholeness. Jesus' goal is for you to be whole. Achieving wholeness takes time. This is because it requires changes on both the inside and outside. Jesus wanted to address what the man was dealing with internally. The same thing for me and you. Jesus had to fix the man's belief. Jesus' response was to change the paralyzed man's mindset. He first wanted the man to believe that he could get up. Jesus wants us to believe it before we receive it. What has held you down in life? Do you think that you can get up from it? If not, then maybe you need to spend some time changing your mindset. The miracles that you have been waiting for are waiting on you; to receive them, you have to change the one thing you can control- your mind.

Now that the man has changed his mindset, Jesus then begins to change his situation. After Jesus explains His authority to the Pharisees, He instructs the man to get up. That's not the only thing Jesus says. He says, "I tell you, get up, take your mat and go home" (Luke 5:24). Jesus not only tells the man to get up, but He also tells the man to take his mat. Why is this important? God renews strength. Jesus wants the paralyzed man to know that he not only has the strength to get up, but he also has the strength to carry the mat. So, the very thing that he was stuck to is the same thing that he now has the power to carry.

The truth is Jesus wants to give you the strength to carry your issues as well. Think deeper. Residents saw the paralyzed man stuck to the mat, probably for years. Seeing the man in the same place would be very discouraging. No one, except his friends, believed that he could get up. How crazy then would it be to see this same man not only walking through the city but carrying the mat as well? Jesus wanted the paralyzed man to serve as an example. Think about other people in the town who were paralyzed. Seeing the man would give them the confidence to stand up as well. God wants you to be an example.

What is your mat?

Now, the big question is, "What's your mat?" Like the man, what is it that you feel like you can never get up from in your life? The mat represents whatever is causing you to be stuck in a season. Whatever it may be, Jesus wants to give you the strength to get up and carry your issues. For me, it was a mixture of things. One example was trying too hard to please people. I was stuck. Yes, in the moment, it felt good! The more I indulged in these distractions, the more I got stuck. I realized that these worldly things were only holding me back from my God-given purpose.

Take time to find your mat. Maybe you are scrolling through social media and get stuck to the number of retweets and likes. Or maybe it is a bad habit that you can't break. Your mat represents whatever is holding you from your purpose. What about your friends? In contrast to the paralyzed man's friends, your friends may be the very people holding you back. Understand, people can be your mat. There are certain people that you have been stuck to that have paralyzed you. You know those "friends" that will keep you on their level. Exactly! They purposely keep you paralyzed so that they can always have someone to fall back on. Don't let this happen to you! Worrying about others will get you stuck, and sometimes separation is key for your growth.

What about religion? Uh, oh, yes, I went there. Religion can become a mat. When I say religion, I am talking about the practice of serving God. There are times where religion can trump a relationship with God. When this happens, we get paralyzed. Many churches with this problem have become paralyzed. At times our beliefs are centered around "Whatever the pastor says," and we rely on our spiritual families to get us through our issues. Trust me; this very thing happened to me.

In college, I was forced to deal with issues in my life, both spiritually and physically. In the past, I relied on my parent's and grandparent's faith to get me through situations. Their faith became my mat. They were not wrong for their prayers and supplication, but it was good to a certain point. They were like the paralyzed man's friends carrying him on the mat. Their faith was necessary, but a time came where the paralyzed man had to have a personal encounter with Jesus. I realized the same was essential for my spiritual development. I had to have my own faith in Jesus to help me through the situations in my life. Jesus began to work through me once I chose to have a personal relationship with Him. Take my life as a note! Don't get stuck to church. The church is necessary, but it can't be your primary focus. God must be the center, and then He will fix your situation.

There are many lessons learned from the story of Jesus and the paralyzed man. In this season, your focus must be on this line, "Get up." Whatever is holding you down, it is time for you to get up. You have been stuck too long. Situations that the enemy has trapped you in along with those we have trapped ourselves with can keep us from God's purpose. Your purpose is waiting for you! It is more significant than you realize! Remember: "they that wait upon the LORD shall renew their strength" (Isaiah 40:31). God wants to renew your strength! For this to happen, you must trust in Him. God wants you to be an example to this generation that you can carry your mat. You may be stuck in whatever season that you are in, but it requires a mindset shift. Center your thoughts around these two words, "Get up!"

Let's dissect the notion of becoming unstuck. I want to help you by giving you some tips on how to get up from whatever is hindering your purpose.

1. Find Your Mat

The first step towards getting up is acknowledging that you are down. Benjamin Disraeli, former Prime Minister of the United Kingdom, says it best: *"To be conscious that you are ignorant of the facts is a great step towards knowledge."* The paralyzed man had to first realize that he needed help. Sometimes we are never able to grow simply because of arrogance. You must accept the fact that you are

---

Religion can become a mat.

---

stuck. Finding your mat requires reflection. What do you keep having to deal with every year? What triggers you? Better yet, who triggers you? Take some time right now and think about what consumes your time unnecessarily. My friend, whatever it may be for you is most likely your mat.

2. Find God

Okay, cool! You have found your mat. The work is not done! You must now understand the person that can get you off of your mat. A lot of times, we miss this step. We settle for people instead of God. We expect people to get us off of our mat, when in reality they are stuck to their mats too! God is the only one who can get you unstuck. Whatever is causing you to be stuck, present it to God. Jesus says, "Your Father knows the things that you need before you ask Him" (Matthew 6:8). I know what you are about to say, "*Then why do I need to tell Him?*" God wants you to understand how much you are dependent on Him. Telling God your issues helps you to realize that He has the power to make your situation better. You cannot be silent in this season! You have been stuck for too long! Take control of your situation by acknowledging that you are stuck, identifying what is causing you to be stuck, and understanding the One who can get you up.

3. Choose Your Squad

What I love most about the story is the faith of the man's friends. If you think about it, his friends were squad goals. They all risked their lives so that their stuck friend could get up again. Whenever they were met with obstacles, they didn't let it stop them from their purpose. The skilled friends even went to a rooftop to get their friend right in front of Jesus. Why is this important? The people you surround yourself with are a reflection of who you are. It's safe to assume that the paralyzed man embodied similar characteristics as his friends.

What does your friend group look like? Do they resemble the paralyzed man's friend group? How can you tell... what is their response when you are paralyzed? Often, you can understand the character of your friends during adversity. The test of adversity is always a gauge of your friend group's mindset. Think about Job's friends. When Job lost everything, his friends reprimanded him because they believed God was punishing him. Despite the criticism, Job remained faithful, and God handled Job's friends. Job more than likely reevaluated his friend group after everything was restored to him.

What's unique about the paralyzed man's friends? First, they pointed him to Jesus. Real friends point you to Jesus whenever you are faced with challenging situations in life. The friends were self-aware and realized they didn't have the skills to fix the man's condition. Some of our friends try to fix all of our issues themselves. When this happens, we get even more stuck. They aren't wrong for trying to help; they are just wrong for thinking that they can do it all. Second, the man's friends were relentless. Once the friend got stuck in the crowd, they tried to find a way at all costs to help their friend. Would your friends do that for you? Some of our friends would probably quit after one obstacle, let alone go up to a roof to help us.

Don't let this be your friend group! Do you have friends like this? Also, don't be that friend! The qualities of the man's friends were the very thing that helped the man to get saved. The Bible says, "When Jesus saw their faith..." (Luke 5:20). The keyword is "their," which means Jesus was not only looking at the faith of the man, but also his friends. Think about your own life. Maybe you have stayed stuck in your situation because God is not waiting for just you to change, but for you to change your friends.

4. Go Home

Don't miss the last thing that Jesus says to the man. He tells the man to "go home" (Luke 5:24). During my first internship, my boss, John Moore, told me something that completely shifted my perspective. He told me, *"Make sure to travel the world and gain exposure to different things, but don't ever forget to come home."* Years later this is something that I still consider with my view of the world.

Our mindset is to get away from home a lot of times, especially if your hometown is small like mine! Leaving your home sometimes is necessary, because it changes your perspective of life. However, the critical thing to remember is to share that perspective. Don't think that the paralyzed man was simply just healed. His mindset shifted because of his encounter with Jesus. He experienced a first-hand miracle. What better person to share the good news of Jesus Christ?

Whenever God brings you out of your struggle, don't forget to share your testimony. Your "home" needs you more than you think. Home is not just about where you grew up. Home is about where you started. The mindset that you started with, the people you started with, and the places where you started all represent your home. Just because you used to sell drugs on the street before God changed your life, doesn't mean you should never go back to those streets. God saved you so you can go back to minister to the same people lost on that very street.

Ultimately, we see this with Jesus. His entire ministry was centered around returning to His home. For us, heaven is also home, and when it is our time, God will take us. God wants us to have this same mindset while on Earth as well. Wherever your home may be, don't forget about it. The common phrase, *"Home is where the heart is,"* should be at the top of your mind. As you grow in life and expand your mind, don't forget your heart. Once you get up from being paralyzed, let God lead you to the place where you are most effective...home.

* * *

What's the Big Idea?

There is one moment that we see Jesus stuck. While others were celebrating Passover, the Romans nailed Jesus to a cross. As Savior of the world, the cross was necessary to fulfill the Old Testament prophecies:

"Dogs surround me, a pack of villains encircles me; they pierce my hands and my feet. All my bones are on display; people stare and gloat over me. They divide my clothes among them and cast lots for my garment" (Psalm 22:16).

The dogs in this prophecy represent the Gentiles (Romans). After the Pharisees accused Jesus of being an insurrectionist, the Pharisees handed Him over to the Romans. For approximately six hours, Jesus was stuck on the cross. I have always wondered, *"Why did Jesus have to struggle for so long on the cross?"* After listening to Dr. Dharius Daniels, lead pastor of Change Church, he offered a hypothesis that helped transform my thinking with this moment. In a sermon on Easter, he said, *"Jesus struggled on the cross to show us how to operate whenever it feels like God has left you hanging."* Has there ever been a moment where you have felt like God has left you hanging? Maybe you felt this way during the pandemic. Perhaps you are stuck relying on unemployment checks trying to figure out why God would put you in this situation when the new decade seemed so promising! It could be the relationships in your life. You feel ready for your soul-mate, but God is making you wait. Whatever this may be, we have all been there! The good news is that Jesus has given us the blue-print of how to operate whenever we are stuck.

1. Look Up, Not Down

Immediately after Jesus was placed on the cross, look at what Jesus says. "Father, forgive them, for they do not know what they are doing" (Luke 23:34). Jesus dealt with so much in that moment. Put yourself in that situation. Many of you would probably be filled with curse words. Don't lie! However, at this moment, we see that Jesus prays. The Bible instructs us to "pray without ceasing" (1 Thessalonians 5:16), and Jesus shows us at this moment how we can. Prayer is not just about getting on your knees and putting your hands together. Prayer is talking to God. You can speak to God with your eyes open even when you are riding in your car. What is most important is that God wants you to talk to Him whenever you deal with adversity.

Before Jesus talks to any man, He speaks to God! James 1:5 states, "If any of you lacks wisdom, let him ask God, who gives generously to all without reproach, and it will be given him." Whenever you feel stuck, who do you talk to? My mother always gets on me about not telling her information about my life. She doesn't have an issue with me sharing important things with others. Her problem is al-ways having to hear something about my life from someone else. To me, it's a much different story. I don't think it is that important, but to my mother it is. I believe that she gets worried that I don't trust her to help me with my situation, but I do. Similarly, God wants you to trust that He can help you whenever you are stuck.

Understand that just because you pray doesn't mean that your situation will automatically change. Trusting in God whenever you are stuck may not free you physically, but it will free you spiritually. You must not get discouraged! Whenever you feel stuck in life, start with prayer. Jesus understood that man would not save Him from this situation, so He chooses to look to the Father. If He had looked down, He would have seen people weeping, mocking Him, and even cursing Him. How depressing! That's what happens whenever we have the wrong perspective. Jesus understood that the cross was symbolic.

To the Romans, Jesus was being lifted up into the air. If you think about it from Jesus' perspective, He was being lifted closer to Heaven. The cross symbolizes Jesus being elevated through His death! Whenever we "die daily" (1 Corinthians 15:31), we are upgraded spiritually as well. Remember, Jesus heals the paralyzed man spiritually first before He tells him to get up. Whenever you are stuck in life, you must choose to look up instead of down in life. Whenever something unfortunate happens in my life, my dad is always the first to say, *"Keep your head up."* Even though I felt terrible about the circumstance, keeping my head up allowed me to focus on the positive instead of the negative. God wants you to do the same whenever you get "stuck" in life. Don't dwell on the negatives of your current circumstance. Look at the positive.

In the Book of Acts, the Sanhedrin (Jewish council) members stoned Stephen to death after they accused him of blasphemy. Whenever Stephen was accused, look at what happens: "But Stephen, full of the Holy Spirit, looked up to Heaven and saw the glory of God, and Jesus standing at the right hand of God. "Look," he said, "I see heaven open and the Son of Man standing at the right hand of God" (Acts 7:55). Stephen was not worried about the thing that man had to say against him. He chose to look up!

Like Jesus, we must continue to take up our cross daily (Luke 9:23). Being a Christian doesn't mean that we are exempt from struggles. However, Jesus promises us peace through adversity. On the cross, Jesus chose to be stuck so that we can be free! You can be free from any circumstance in your life that seems to be holding you hostage. To experience that freedom, you must fix your focus. Whatever your situation may be, Jesus can fix it! Don't focus on all of the people laughing and persecuting. Look up! Fix your eyes on Jesus.

2. Silence is Deadly

One of the lessons that I have learned dealing with people is everything doesn't require a response. The enemy uses people to make you angry to make you act out of character. Whenever this happens, you lose focus on the overall objective because you have given all of your energy to everyone else's opinions. This happens the most whenever you are paralyzed! Think back to the paralyzed man. Everyone probably had their idea about what he should do. Thank God he had a great friend group that led him to Jesus! You have to be careful of the voices that you respond to. The more people you allow to give you their opinions, the more likely you will make an irrational decision. Look how Jesus handles this!

Jesus wasn't the only one crucified on that Friday. On the left and right of Jesus, two criminals were sentenced to death. The two men were forced to carry their cross, and they were positioned to the left and right of Jesus. On one side, there was a man who mocked Jesus and questioned His abilities. Then on the other side, you had a man who recognized His authority and value. Maybe you have both kinds of people in your social circle. The reason the two men treated Jesus differently wasn't about their personality, but their perspective. Jesus was seen differently by the two men, literally and figuratively. You must know that the people around you treat you differently in your life because they see you differently. One of the men just saw Jesus' skills and abilities, but the other recognized His anointing. People can realize your skills but still not recognize your value. Issues happen whenever you spend your time and energy trying to educate these people about your importance. Let's analyze what Jesus does when He is confronted:

One of the criminals who hung there hurled insults at him, "Aren't you the Messiah? Save yourself and us!" But the other criminal rebuked him. "Don't you fear God," he said, "since you are under the same sentence? We are punished justly, for we are getting what our deeds deserve. But this man has done nothing wrong." Then he said, "Jesus, remember me when you come into your kingdom." Jesus answered him, "Truly I tell you, today you will be with me in paradise" (Luke 23:39).

How would you respond to this kind of insult? Put yourself in Jesus' place. After all He had done for the world and all you get in return is mockery! Better yet, Jesus was about to die to save the same man that was mocking Him! It had to be so demoralizing to listen to him insult Jesus in this way. Hold on! Look back at the verse. The man spits multiple insults. Then, the other man immediately rebukes him. What is missing? Jesus' response. The next time that we hear Jesus talk is to the man who begs Jesus to remember him. Why didn't Jesus say anything to the man who was insulting Him? The man needed no response.

Now don't think that Jesus didn't respond. Johnathan Carroll said it best when he says, *"Not responding is a response."* Jesus responds, but not in the way that we expect. Some of the most potent statements Jesus ever makes had no words. Understand, if Jesus didn't need to respond to everything, then neither should you! One of the things my great-grandmother always used to say is "pass 'em," which means you demonstrate an elevated behavioral standard. No response sometimes is the best response. This doesn't mean that you don't respond to anything, but you don't have to respond to everything! Whenever you are stuck in life, don't let the mockers keep you down. Jesus was mindful that His purpose was much bigger than answering the insults of others. Understand! If Jesus had focused on the man's insults, He probably would have tried to show that He had the power to get down from the cross. He would have proved a point while missing His purpose.

How many times have you been in this situation? The man on the cross already knew the answer to the questions that he was asking Jesus. All the man wanted was to get Jesus to act out of character. However, Jesus realized there were bigger things He had to do. Are you more concerned about winning the battles in your life or the war? There will be many people who have something to say. If you focus on the insults, then it takes your focus away from purpose. In most situations in your life, your most important weapon is your silence. Remember, silence is deadly. The enemy's goal is for you to be distracted. Silence kills distractions. Think about it. You don't hear from the thief that insults Jesus again. This doesn't mean you shouldn't ever speak up! You must be strategic and know when to be silent. What you don't say is just as important as what you do say!

3. Waiting to Exhale

When I was in elementary school, we would play this game to see who could hold their breath the longest. So, a bunch of us gathered around the playground at recess. One person counted the time, and then the competitors stood in the middle of the circle. Ready! Set! Go! I pulled in as much air as I could and closed my mouth. Everybody around me was cheering. Kids were dropping left and right. I looked, it was me, and this small kid left. I started to feel myself wanting to breathe, and he just looked at me and smiled. Seconds later, I gave up. I started coughing and tried to breathe as much as I could. As I looked up, the boy was still holding his breath. He opened his mouth for about two minutes, and all of the kids started to cheer for him. Looking back on that moment, I laugh thinking about how silly and dangerous it was. However, it serves as a great segway in our third topic of discussion.

Life is filled with pressure. There are moments in life where you feel like you are holding your breath. You have inhaled the worries of this world. This could be the bills, relationship drama, or even trouble at work. Everything is working against you, and there seems to be no one that you can talk to. You feel paralyzed. When this happens, you feel as if the weight of the world is on you. Many times, we "hold our breath" in life to prove a point. Holding your breath is a signal that you are trying to do things on your own. Every time someone is worried, what is the first thing that people always say? Breathe. The act of breathing is a two-step process. Everything you take in; you must let out. When you breathe, you are trusting in God's handiwork within you to continue to give you life. You try to take on the world yourself whenever you hold your breath. Issues arise when you take things in but don't let them out. You refuse to give your problems to God. You must realize that you are not Jesus, nowhere close, and you must understand that He is the only One ever to overcome the world. Despite all of His power and authority, Jesus even chooses to let go.

Still on the cross, Jesus continues to hold on to dear life as He is being crucified on the cross. Hours had gone by to what was now afternoon—nails in his hand(s) and feet, a crown of thorns on His head. What endurance He had to have to withstand such torture. Then came the moment of truth. Jesus yelled, "Father into your hands I commit my spirit" (Luke 23:44). After saying these words, He breathes one last time before giving up His spirit.

Jesus bottled up thirty-three years of healing and performing miracles into one last breath. We know that this isn't the end of Jesus' story. However, this is a crucial moment in the life of Jesus. His last breath symbolized Jesus was giving up all His issues to the Father. Everything Jesus dealt with on Earth was now given to God. We must do the same! This is the essence of carrying your cross. The idea is that we let go of our problems and give our lives up to God!

The reality is that God is waiting for you to exhale. You have been paralyzed for too long. Everyone in this world is holding onto something. Whatever "it" maybe, it is no secret to God. He knows what you are going through. He knows that you feel stuck. All God wants you to do is trust in Him.

Whenever Jesus heals the paralyzed man, it was because the men decided to come to Him! In this season, you may feel burdened and weary, but Jesus, in these moments He says, "Come to Me" (Matthew 11:28). You must trust in God, even when you feel like you have hit rock bottom. God will pick you back up! You only begin to grow whenever you let go! Letting go doesn't mean neglecting your issues and doing whatever. You trust that you cannot handle all of your problems yourself but have given it to the One who can! Think about it. If Jesus hadn't let go, He would've delayed His resurrection. Same thing for you! God is looking to resurrect some things in your life, but He is waiting for you to hand them to Him.

Activating purpose starts with getting up. Whenever the world hits you hard, you get paralyzed. Whenever you are paralyzed, you must focus on the One who has overcome the world, Jesus Christ! God will give you the strength to get back up again! Your purpose is too great to be paralyzed! God wants your life to change! First, you must believe that He can change it. Focus on getting up from your mat and walking into God's purpose for your life!

Thought: Whenever you begin to feel like your struggle will never change, you are paralyzed. God can bring you out of any situation, but you must start by changing your mindset.

6

The Purpose Battlefield

On October 30, 1974, Muhammad Ali defeated George Foreman in one of the most notable boxing matches in history known as "The Rumble in the Jungle." Many sports broadcasters predicted a George Foreman win in a knockout. At the beginning of the fight, Foreman got off to a quick start by landing a couple of vicious punches out of the gate. The force behind Foreman's hit made it seem like Ali's body would not be able to make it after a couple of rounds. However, as the fights progressed, everyone saw Ali's strategy. His goal was to use his elusiveness while also causing Foreman to lose energy. The plan was executed perfectly. After four rounds, Foreman's punches went from ferocious to lackluster. He struggled to keep up with Ali. In the eighth round, George Foreman grew weary, and Ali began his attack. Ali landed a couple of punches to the head, causing Foreman to stumble backward. Then, BOOM! Ali landed a blow to the head, and George Foreman fell to the ground. The crowd went crazy! The referee began to count "1... 2... 3..." The fight was over. Muhammad Ali won by knockout, and it is still remembered as one of the "greatest fights of the 20th Century."

Watching this fight on television made me realize something important. Sometimes, God requires us to fight for our purpose. What do I mean? Well, think back to the story of Jacob (Genesis 25). He was fighting even when he was in the womb. Jacob fights with his brother, Esau, in Rachel's womb. Rachel is wondering why the wrestling was happening. Then God tells her, "Two nations are in your womb, and two peoples from within you will be separated; one people will be stronger than the other, and the older will serve the younger" (Genesis 25:23). The wrestling between Jacob and Esau has continued between the two nations even after their deaths. One of the iconic moments in the Bible happens when Jacob wrestles with God. Through wrestling, God blesses Jacob with his new identity: Israel.

In our life, we go through battles. God shows us through Jacob's life that battles will be present throughout our life. Wrestling may come in many different forms. There will always be issues that force us to wrestle in life. The battles may not be to the extent of "The Rumble in the Jungle," but there are events that we go through in life that make us feel like we are in a ring. Despite Ali's championship status, people still counted Ali out because of Foreman's sheer size and strength. Similarly, there are situations in our life that can scare us because of the appearance. Some battles become too large to handle, and it begins to overwhelm us. God never put us through any battle that we can't win. However, the enemy will try to make situations seem different than what it looks like. The enemy's strategy is to make things bigger than what it seems to distract you from your purpose.

Let's jump to an infamous story where the enemy uses size to intimidate people. In 1 Samuel, we are introduced to a young man named David. Many of us know the story about David and Goliath, but before we detail that battle, there are other battles in David's life that he is forced to overcome. David was thought to be an illegitimate child. Some scholars suggest that Jesse was not David's biological father. So, out of the womb, he is forced to overcome adversity. David writes about his illegitimacy, saying, "I am become a stranger unto my brethren, and an alien unto my mother's children" (Psalm 69:8). He spends most of his life as a shepherd alone in the field. While his father, Jesse, spent time building relationships with his seven other sons, David was alone in the field surrounded by sheep. So, we see that David's first battle starts in his own household. Even though David could not build a true relationship with his physical father, that did not stop him from connecting with his Heavenly Father. So in the field, David served both his physical and spiritual father. He tended to his sheep serving his earthly father and wrote psalms to connect with his Heavenly Father. David does not grow up in the most favorable environments, but he still continues to praise God despite the adversity.

David gives us insight into how we can overcome the battles in our life. Amid our battles, praise is the weapon that will confuse the enemy. Praise was the weapon that frees Paul and Silas out of prison. God is looking to free you from the things that have been holding you hostage. Our praise is the thing that activates purpose. The angels in Heaven begin to move on our behalf whenever we praise. Look at what David goes on to say, "My mouth is filled with your praise declaring your splendor all day long" (Psalm 71:8). Every moment of our life should be filled with praise, no matter good or bad days. Often, we are in positions like David, where we may have been struggling with problems in our own household or attempting to find purpose in our lives. David chose not to dwell on his problems but focus on God. In his trouble, he thanks God. The same thing should apply to us as well! Why let our problems control us when God - who is on our side - controls our problems? Let your praise be the answer to your fears!

David faithfully spends seasons serving. God saw his faithfulness and told the prophet, Samuel, to go anoint David as king. So David's service led to his elevation. Often, we focus on pleasing others and making ourselves known to people to increase our status. However, David was not focused on people, but on God. David's focus allowed him to inherit the kingdom God had already prepared for him. If you want to elevate in this season, you must start by serving others. God wants to see if you are faithful in your "field" before He places you in your "palace."

Samuel comes and anoints David as the next king of Israel. David can wear all the jewels and inherit all of the world's riches now, right? Wrong. David gets anointed, and the next thing that God calls him to do is... you guessed it... serve. He continues to serve as a shepherd. Suddenly, the current king, Saul, confronts an evil spirit because of his disobedience. Saul's attendants search for someone to ease their king's spiritual warfare.

During their search, one of the attendants said, "I have seen a son of Jesse of Bethlehem who knows how to play the lyre. He is a brave man and a warrior. He speaks well and is a fine-looking man. And the Lord is with him" (1 Samuel 16:18). David is a simple field servant, yet other people saw different qualities in him! God saw him as more than a shepherd. There were more dimensions to him.

You are also multidimensional. Stop seeing yourself as one-dimensional when God sees you differently! So, David leaves home to serve Saul and plays his lyre. The same lyre he uses to write songs of praise is the same instrument he uses to confront Saul's evil spirits. The evil spirit leaves when David plays. There was anointing with David's praise, and his anointing had the power to drive out evil spirits. The same power is within you, and like David, it requires a relationship with God.

Wait, but David is king? Why does he have to serve Saul when God calls him to be a king? The answer is this, God spends those

---

God wants to see if you are faithful in your "field" before He places you in your "palace."

---

seasons preparing David for the kingdom. David spends the first part of his life learning, by taking care of sheep. God spends time teaching David more about leadership. David learns many lessons from Saul. Maybe, indirectly. However, David still learns a lot from serving under Saul. Saul's mistakes were simply meant to educate David on leadership. God provides the warning signs for David so that he doesn't make the same mistakes. Just as God placed David in environments to learn, the same applies to you. That boss that you dread going to work for is someone you can learn from. God is showing you how not to operate once you are CEO of your own company. Don't despise being in the background. You are learning! There are lessons in each season in life. Some seasons are meant for maturing and preparing. It is the response to these seasons that will determine the trajectory of your destiny.

Now let's jump to Goliath. We all know the story. David defeats Goliath. However, there are so many details leading up to the story that cannot go unnoticed. The Philistines have declared war against the Israelites. The Israelites have consistently defeated the Philistines. However, this time the Philistines introduced their champion, Goliath, to the battle. Goliath's physical stature frightens the Israelites. Many of the Israelite soldiers hide when Goliath challenges them to a duel. They hid for forty days looking for someone brave enough to face this foe.

Meanwhile, David is serving in the fields while the war is taking place. His brothers are fighting in the battle. Jesse tasks David with checking on his brothers and sending them food. However, Jesse doesn't know that he is actually sending David to defeat the

Philistines. David arrives and overhears Goliath's taunting demands to the Israelites. Everyone else is hiding and David begins to question why they are afraid. He tells the soldiers, "Who is this uncircumcised Philistine that he should defy the armies of the living God?" (1 Samuel 17:26). David doesn't even bother calling him by his name! David continues to speak to the soldiers about defeating Goliath, and his brother begins yelling at him. His brother, Eliab, angrily says, "Why have you come down here?" (1 Samuel 17:28).

Surprise.

The first person to stop David from his assignment was a family member. We often have family members who are holding us back from purpose. Sometimes the destinations God has called us to don't match anything your family has ever done. No one in David's family has ever defeated a giant! However, God called David to be the first. Eliab might have been angry because he was trying to protect David. However, even protection can be a limitation. Remember how God took Abraham away from his father's house to fulfill His intended purpose. God sometimes has to do the same for us. However, when family challenges us, our mentality should emulate David's because he wouldn't let family stop him from his assignment.

Fight for Purpose, NOT Potential

Whenever David speaks about Goliath, he is immediately met with a dilemma. The Israelites create incentives for anyone who defeats Goliath. They say, "The king will give great wealth to the man who kills him," "He will give him his daughter in marriage," and "will exempt his family from taxes in Israel" (1 Samuel 17:25). The problem with incentives is they are not guaranteed. Paulo Coelho talks about this in his book, *The Alchemist.* Coelho states, "If you start out by promising what you don't even have yet, you'll lose your desire to work toward getting it." This applies right here in David's life, and currently where you may be. There are a lot of tangible promises that society makes to us about our situations. Things like *"money is the way to happiness"* or *"the better your job, the more people will respect you."* We often succumb to society's claims, but what happens when money doesn't result in happiness, or you get the top job but your co-workers conspire against you? See too often, we chase after potential but ignore purpose! In this case, David was not worried about worldly riches, but he focused on protecting the Israelites. Once a shepherd, always a shepherd.

In life, we can't get caught up in potential. Our focus is typically, "God, I want to be a millionaire" or "I want this job so I can get this corner office." In life or death situation, will any of those things matter? At the end of your life, the million dollars and that luxurious corner office will not make a difference. Life or death is what the Israelites were facing during this time. Goliath challenges the Israelites to a one-on-one duel. He exclaims, "If he is able to fight and kill me, we will become your subjects; but if I overcome him and kill him, you will become our subjects and serve us" (1 Samuel 17:9).

This is more than just any typical battle. The battle will determine the future of the Israelites. If David were to lose, then the Israelites would have been in the same predicament as they were in Egypt. At this moment, David's focus was not on his potential. He wasn't worried about position, wealth, or any other reward. For David, his only focus was to protect the Israelites from the Philistines. David was a true shepherd. He remembers his purpose in life is to be a protector. All of those people in David's eyes were his sheep, and Philistines were the lions and bears that he had to defeat in the field. In David's eyes, just because the environment might have changed, he still had to fulfill the same purpose.

In the face of this giant, David remembers his why. He recalled that God had anointed him to be king. Through God calling him to be king, David realizes that if he hasn't become king, then Goliath was simply just a steppingstone to the kingdom. Goliath had to go! God wouldn't have brought David that far just for him to be defeated. God would not bring Moses all the way out of Egypt just for him to be blocked by the Red Sea. Just as for David and Moses, God has not brought you this far for you to be defeated by whatever "giant" is in front of you. This may not be a physical giant. Goliath represents the thing that intimidates you. For instance, your giant may represent depression or anxiety. What is your Goliath?

If you have been hiding from your Goliath, then this is for you! God wants you to go TO the battlefield. Oftentimes, we run away from our problems. Whatever you run from, whether it be alcohol, drugs, or social media, God wants you to trust in Him! Once you place your trust in Him, you will see how small your giants are compared to our God. The key to overcoming your giants is to remember your why. Remember the promises that God has made for you! The giants are simply obstacles to test your faith. You are called for greater! David had the advantage over Goliath because God was on his side. You have the same advantage! Start focusing on God whenever you are challenged by your giants. Then, watch how God helps you win the victory!

Put on your clothes

As David prepares to go into the "ring" with Goliath, he is forced to deal with an unsupportive corner. Saul calls for any soldier that is willing to face Goliath to come forward and fight. David comes along to face Goliath. Instead of giving David any advice on the battle, Saul gives David his armor. "Then Saul dressed David in his own tunic" (1 Samuel 17:38). David tries to put on Saul's clothes and

---

Goliath represents the thing that intimidates you.

---

walks around uncomfortably. He tells Saul, "I cannot go in there" (1 Samuel 17:39). There are situations where people try to make us put on their armor to fight our battles. Not just physical armor. Some people try to tell you how to go about facing "Goliaths" in life. We will let our friends, family, or the Internet tell us how to defeat giants they have never faced before.

Don't believe me? Just look at what happens whenever we get sick. We will look at our symptoms and immediately run to Google. WebMD will say the symptoms, and it will make us think that we have pneumonia. It is probably just a common cold! Now, if you really are sick, please go see a doctor! All I am saying is that sometimes we settle for what everyone else says about our situation instead of what God has said. God saw fit to anoint David without an army or sword. He didn't have any armor or shield when he defeated the lions and bears to protect his sheep. Don't rely on everyone else's opinion on how to win YOUR battles. David felt uncomfortable for this reason...Saul has never been through what David was about to do. Saul had never defeated any giants, so how could he tell him what clothes he should wear for the battle? If all your friends are single, why are they trying to clothe your relationships with their opinions? You have everything you need right now to defeat your giants!

This applies to family as well. Don't let family force you into things that you are uncomfortable with. Your circle can face its giants their own way, but God has created a unique pathway for you to defeat yours. God wants you to be you! That's why He created you the way that He did. God has designed you to be great!

The Enemy Has Your Sword

Here it goes! In one corner, we have the Israelite's representative, David, and in the other corner the Philistine representative, Goliath. David goes down to the valley to face Goliath. I'd imagine that the closer David got to Goliath, the taller and taller Goliath became. However, David does something profound. Goliath mocks David by calling him a "stick" and tells him that he will give his flesh to "birds and the wild animals" (1 Samuel 17:44). Then David says, "... I'll strike you down and cut off your head" (1 Samuel 17:46). What a bold statement! It is interesting that David says that he will cut off Goliath's head. Stones don't cut off heads, so why would he say that? The answer is this: David didn't come to battle with a sword, but he knew that he was leaving with one.

Ultimately, David defeats Goliath and goes on to kill "tens of thousands" (1 Samuel 18:7). He becomes one of the greatest warriors ever to walk the face of the earth. What does he use? David uses the sword that was in Goliath's hands. Consider this, Goliath HAD to give up his sword to David. In this season, there will be some things that the enemy will have to hand over to you to take you into your purpose.

David's purpose was wrapped in Goliath's hands. Likewise, this strategy of the enemy is what goes on in our life. The enemy's trick is to try and mask your purpose with your giants. The giants come into your life whenever there is a greater purpose on the other side. Stop looking at your giants! Start looking for what the enemy is trying to hide from you. The enemy may try to make you depressed just to cover up something God has planned for you. The thing that troubles your relationships, your business, your health is the enemy's last attempt to keep you from opening the door to your destiny. The enemy wants you to focus on Goliath, but God wants you to focus on Him.

There was a kingdom waiting for David on the other side of Goliath! David remembers Samuel coming to anoint him, reminding him that the Lord has chosen him. He realizes that Goliath is simply just a checkpoint on his journey. David knew as long as he trusted God, that he couldn't die there. You won't die in your battles! The word God has spoken over your life will still come to pass. Remember your oil. God protects who He has anointed, and even a giant can't touch His chosen people.

I know you are probably wondering why I made the reference to "The Rumble in the Jungle" earlier. Well, there are a lot of similarities between both battles. An uncommon strategy was used in both fights, and the underdog came out on top. David grabs a stone and winds it around in his slingshot. He releases the stone, and it hits Goliath smack dab in the forehead. In the eighth-round, Ali takes a similar approach and presents vicious blows to the head knocking out George Foreman. Both Ali and David defeat their opponents by striking them in the head! The same thing must happen for you in this season. I am not saying go and punch your enemies in the face. Ha! However, I am saying that it is time to start addressing the giants in your life head-on. Stop avoiding your problems and acknowledge it. David never would've gotten the kingdom if he would've avoided Goliath. You must realize those giants in your life are no match for the God on your side! This season is your opportunity to get what the enemy has been trying to hold from you. For David, it was his kingdom, what is it for you?

In middle school, one of the worst things that someone could ever say about you is, *"They don't know how to fight."* Most of the time, that meant that you had either lost a fight or simply looked as if you could not fight. Even though this was such an insult in grade school, knowing how to fight is very important. Not just physically, but also spiritually! Many people try to deal with battles in their life without

> **David didn't come to battle with a sword, but he knew that he was leaving with one.**

knowing how to fight them. You are already at a disadvantage when you don't know how to fight, and you are more likely to get beat up. Don't let the enemy beat you up! Let's dive deeper into the "Rumble in The Jungle," to get more insight into how to fight your battles in life.

1. LEARN YOUR OPPONENT

Muhammad Ali uses the "rope-a-dope" strategy not to avoid George Foreman, but to learn from him. Many of the rounds, he was simply evaluating Foreman's strategy to win. Ali sacrificed rounds to evaluate Foreman. There are seasons in our life where it may feel like we are losing to the enemy. However, God is just trying to educate you.

Wisdom comes with experience. Yes! You may take many blows in life and have to deal with many difficult situations. Don't see it as you are losing. Thank God that you are learning! The enemy came out swinging ever since the garden. Many leaders throughout the history of Israel may have lost their rounds, but Jesus came to deliver the knockout punch! God is setting you up for the knockout punch for your enemies. Know that studying the Bible allows you not only to see the goodness of God but also exploits the tricks of the enemy. Understand the stories and lessons are meant to teach you! Once you learn your enemy, he will have no tricks that can affect you! This is one of the many things my grandma knows so well. She can spot the devil's tricks from a mile away. She can pray the enemy out of any situation. However, she spent many years of learning and building her relationship with God. The same applies to us!

Take your time to study, and you will be able to withstand any attack of the enemy.

2. DON'T BELIEVE THE HYPE

Even though Ali is considered the greatest heavyweight fighter of all time, he actually came into the fight versus Foreman as the underdog. Many boxing experts projected Foreman to win by knockout. Ali didn't let the hype phase him, he let it fuel him! Many people on the battlefield probably treated David the same way as Ali. The Israelite soldiers cowered at the giant in front of them. The soldiers were perhaps discussing amongst themselves how they already lost the battle. Even Saul told David, "You are not able to go out against this Philistine and fight him; you are only a young man, and he has been a warrior from his youth" (1 Samuel 17:33). David's own captain didn't even have faith!

A lot of these same things will happen to you as you fight the battles in life. People will say things about you to convince you to second guess yourself. Understand this! Saul wasn't wrong with his comments to David. However, he was looking through his lens, not God's lens. People may say things about you that might be true. Don't let it deter you from your purpose! The hype is simply just a distraction.

Here's one of the enemy's favorite strategies...lying. If what people are saying doesn't align with what God is saying, it is most likely the enemy trying to distract you with his many lies. Your purpose is too essential to quit because of what people say about you. They don't understand the level of your anointing. Go into the battles of your life confidently, not because of what man says, but because of what God says.

3. KNOCK 'EM OUT

There is one more similarity between David and Muhammad Ali that I would like to point out. Both went for the kill. Muhammad Ali defies the odds and knocks out Foreman. Ali knocks out the very person everyone thought was going to knock him out. Similarly, David knocks out Goliath! Afterward, he takes Goliath's sword and cuts off the giant's head. It is crucial in our battles that we don't settle for merely surviving, but we focus on thriving. We may overcome things in our lives, but if we don't eliminate them, it could come back in another season. This may be an addiction or a toxic relationship. God wants you completely free from your issues. However, sometimes we can become lazy and not truly address our problems. The enemy uses laziness to keep you in cycles. Don't settle.

What are you fighting in this season? What is causing depression to come back into your life? Is there something in your life that feels unconquerable? It must not know about the God you serve! It is time to defeat your giants! It's not only about defeating them but eliminating them. To accomplish this, you must first address your giants head-on, then, the power of God will destroy every force that has attempted to attack you.

* * *

What's the Big Idea?

Who said that Jesus never had to fight? Jesus had to participate in the greatest fight of all time. The battle we see between David and Goliath was just a precursor to Jesus and the enemy in the wilderness. Most of the battles fought in the New Testament were spiritual. Like David, no one ever expected Jesus, a carpenter from Nazareth, to fight any battle. However, the spiritual warfare that Jesus endures in the wilderness is what ultimately prepares Him for ministry. Jesus understood that walking in purpose required Him to

fight in the wilderness. The Spirit leads Him into the wilderness after He is baptized by John the Baptist. After Jesus is baptized, God
says, "This is my Son, whom I love; with him I am well pleased"
(Matthew 3:17). Nevertheless, Jesus still goes to be tested.

Don't ignore this!

The greatest battle that you will ever face will be against your
greatest opponent - yourself. Validation doesn't exempt you from
preparation. God has called you to be great! Even though you have
been validated by God, you must still prepare for whatever you are
called to do. Like Jesus, preparation requires a test. God wants to
prepare not only your mind, but also your heart. Let's take a closer
look at the battle.

Similar to Goliath, what makes the enemy seem so large is the
threat of death. The goal of the enemy is to destroy. If he can destroy
you, then his hope is that your purpose will be destroyed. Understand, the enemy's desire is to turn you away from God. During
the enemy's fall from Heaven, there were angels that fell with him
(Luke 10:18). Since there is a limited number of angels, the enemy
uses them strategically. The goal is not to attack just anyone, he
strategically attacks leaders. There is a reason you have been faced
with so many attacks. You are a leader! The enemy understands
your impact and wants to attack you first. When it came to Jesus,
the enemy understood that he had to attack Him personally. The
enemy understood the impact Jesus would have with His ministry,
which is why the enemy tried to stop it even before it went public!

When I was younger, I met a spirited champion of Science,
Technology, Engineering, and Mathematics (STEM), Dr. Calvin
Mackie. He told a story of lions and cheetahs that I have never forgotten. In the wild, lions and cheetahs go through a dispute that is
similar to Jesus and the enemy. We all know that lions are the king
of the jungle. However, lions feel threatened by the cheetah because
they can run faster. Cheetahs can run almost 25 miles per hour

faster. This means they can get to prey or any other food source first. In order to eliminate the threat, lions make an effort to kill cheetah cubs before they can grow up. The lions kill the cheetah cubs to eliminate the competition. Similarly, the enemy sees you as a threat. The enemy understands that your ministry, through whatever industry, will expand God's kingdom. So, he tries to attack you before you even start. This is why Herod tries to kill Jesus when He was just a baby. Whatever God has called you to build will endure its hardest seasons in its infancy.

Since we looked at the opponents, now let's look at the setting. The battle takes place in the wilderness. Whenever Jesus arrives, the enemy doesn't bother to introduce himself. Why? They both know each other very well. Jesus is well aware of the schemes of the enemy, which is why the wilderness was so important. Jesus comes to win the battle that the Israelites lost! In the Old Testament, the Israelites spent forty years in the wilderness and during that time they struggled spiritually. In a similar fashion, Jesus willingly puts Himself in the same struggle as the Israelites. The difference is, what took the Israelites forty years to overcome, Jesus solves in forty days. Where David had to go down to the valley to face Goliath (1 Samuel 17:28), Jesus goes up to the mountain to face the enemy. Just as a reminder, the battle between David and Goliath represents much of the physical battles that we face in our lives.

In the wilderness, the battle between Jesus and the enemy represents the battles that we face spiritually. We see that David calls on the name of the Lord as he goes to fight Goliath, and Jesus also focuses on the Lord. It is important to understand that we must call on the name of the Lord no matter the circumstance. In David's case, his confession allowed him to defeat Goliath with a stone. For Jesus, it forced the enemy to flee. The Lord wants to help you in the same way with your battles! Heaven comes down on our behalf to fight our battles. Whenever you deal with spiritual battles, you must give your problems up to the Lord! God will then fight the unseen battles so that the enemy will be forced to flee.

Now that you have been introduced to the opponents and learned about the setting. Let's get into the battle. Jesus and the enemy face each other for three rounds in the wilderness. With each round, there are three different ways that the enemy tries to turn Jesus away from God. I want to analyze the enemy's tricks to help you navigate through the spiritual warfare that you will endure in your life.

1. Bread and Stones

Naturally, after forty days in the wilderness, Jesus was hungry. Not having anything to eat or drink for a day is hard for me, nevermind more than five and a half weeks! The flesh of Jesus had to plead for some nourishment! Of course, the enemy tried to use Jesus' hunger as an entryway to His heart. The enemy proposed to Jesus, "If you are the Son of God, tell these stones to become bread" (Matthew 4:6). Wait. What? Look how the enemy started this sentence *If you are the Son of God...* Moments before Jesus went to the wilderness, doesn't God inform the world that Jesus was "His Son" and "with whom I am well pleased?" If God told everyone (including the enemy), why would the enemy say this to Jesus? Here is the answer... the first move of the enemy is to make you question yourself. Think about it. Where else do we see this pattern? The Garden of Eden. "Did God really say, 'You must not eat from any tree in the garden?" Eve fails, but Jesus succeeds. Why? Jesus never loses focus. Right now, you may feel as if you are losing the battles in your life. Fix your focus! Jesus replies, "It is written: 'Man shall not live on bread alone, but on every word that comes from the mouth of God" (Matthew 4:4). Eve attempts to answer the enemy's questions herself, but Jesus answers these questions with Scripture. The enemy's intention is for you to answer yourself because your mindset is limited. Since you are so crucial to the Kingdom of God, the enemy has been watching you throughout your life. He has observed your every move during these times and has taken note of all your weaknesses. The enemy is very creative and knows how to attack. While you are playing checkers, the enemy is playing chess! What would happen if you went to a chess tournament with only knowledge of how to play checkers? You would never win! This is exactly what happens when we try to fight our own battles. Therefore, we must hand our life over to the greatest chess champion. Yes, you guessed it... God!

Let's go back to the statement the enemy makes to Jesus, but let's analyze the why behind the statement. Jesus was hungry, and the enemy attempted to try and take advantage. The enemy understood that he couldn't physically kill Jesus. Therefore, he wanted to steer Him away from purpose. To do this, he tried to make Jesus hungry for the wrong things. You must be aware of this in your own life. One of the common mantras today is "*Get that bread!*" This term is associated with money. Be careful! The "bread" the enemy tries to distract you with could be money. God specifically tells us to "keep your life free from the love of money" (Hebrews 13:5). Since money is the means of living today, it can be distracting! However, focusing on the money shows that you are putting your trust in money instead of God. The Bible says, "Blessed are those who hunger and thirst for righteousness, for they will be filled" (Matthew 5:6). Notice that the verse didn't say that you won't get hungry. In life, there will be times that you are in need and are hungry for answers to life's questions. In these situations, you must channel that hunger away from the world and to God.

Let's look more into the bread and stones. Stones represent the permanent things in your life, and bread symbolizes whatever is temporary. Take a moment to think about the "bread" and "stones" in your life. The enemy's primary objective is to replace the permanent things in your life with whatever is temporary. Why do you think so many marriages end in divorce because of an affair? Relationships built on strong foundations broken by sex and lust. Doesn't this sound exactly like the enemy? Jesus could have easily turned the stone into bread. The only thing that Jesus turning stone into bread would have proven is that Jesus gave into His fleshly desires instead of trusting in God.

In our lives, whenever we temporarily give in to our flesh, it means that we are choosing to trust in ourselves instead of God. Whenever Jesus says, *"Man shall not live on bread alone,"* He is not saying that you can't enjoy temporary things in life. It just can't be what you solely rely on. Then Jesus says, "but from every word that comes from the mouth of God" (Matthew 4:4). God's Word is our bread! Whenever the enemy tries to urge you to replace the "stones" in your life, know that God gives you all of the "bread" you need.

To be clear, the enemy presented options, but the decision is your choice. Whenever Jesus replies to the enemy with Scripture, it wasn't meant for God. It was to encourage Himself. Fill your mind with Scripture. Whenever the hunger comes, you will be able to use these scriptures to help your endurance. Don't turn your stones into bread! Keep trusting in the Lord, and He will provide all of the nourishment that you need!

2. Daredevil Ends with Evil

Growing up, I knew a kid who was the definition of a daredevil. When we played, he would tell me everything he wanted to try that day. We built ramps for our bikes, went fishing, and played video

---

Stones represent the permanent things in your life, and bread symbolizes whatever is temporary.

---

games. One day, he came over to the house and said, *"Do you wanna go mud bogging?"* Not having a clue of what that would consist of, I was apprehensive. He told me to follow him, and we would have fun.

After agreeing, I followed him to this swamp-like area at the back of our neighborhood. I had never been to this part of the neighborhood. Following his lead, I watched him go through the swamp to the pile of mud. Then, out of nowhere, I felt mud on my face. He rode his bike as fast as he could through the mud. Once he finished, he yelled back to me to follow suit. I sped through the mud and got mud all over my bike and my clothes. We proceeded to do it again, about ten times and pedaled back home. I came back to the house covered in mud, and my mother was furious! I looked around for him, and he was nowhere to be found. My mom took me under the garage and told me to take my clothes off to be washed. As you can probably guess, my dad wasn't too happy as well whenever he got home.

The fact that I am still alive should tell you I never went "mud-bogging" again. There were many lessons that I learned that day, but one stood out to me. The main lesson that I learned was I had to figure out who I was. Amid all the yelling, my mother told me, *"You are not the same person as him!"* which really resonated with me. I realized that I just wanted to fit in, and I had no clue of my own identity.

Similarly, you may be dealing with trying to fit in. From this story, the critical thing to understand is that trying to fit in can get you into a mess. Looking back on this moment, enlightened me about the next way that the enemy tries to attack us. After the enemy failed to get Jesus to turn the stone into bread, he didn't quit. You must understand that endurance is key to spiritual warfare. Many people celebrate getting through situations in their life when the battle is not over. Jesus understands and remains aware of the traps that the enemy has set forth. The enemy took Jesus to the highest point in the temple and said, "If you are the Son of God", he said, "Throw yourself down." What a bold proposal! The enemy even references Scripture when making his proposal: "He will command his angels concerning you, and they will lift you up in their hands, so that you will not strike your foot against a stone" (Psalm 91:11-12).

You must remember that the enemy knows the Bible too! The enemy will try and bend Scripture to fit with his plan to turn you away from God. This is why you must not only understand the Bible, but you must also have a relationship with the One who made it! Understand, bad doctrine is one of the enemy's weapons. People have used the Bible to justify a lot of evil in the world. Throughout history, people have used the Bible to justify slavery, sexism, and many other issues that have plagued the world. You must let the Holy Spirit lead you through the Word so that God can give you the proper interpretation of the text. Revelation eliminates misinterpretation!

How does Jesus combat this attack? He gives the enemy more Scripture. He says, "It is also written: 'Do not put the Lord your God to the test'" (Matthew 4:7). Jesus gives us the key to overcoming the enemy's Biblical tricks that will be helpful to you. Jesus says, "It is also written." Whenever you spot bad doctrine, it is usually a person spinning a certain verse or using a subject in the Bible to add relevance to their arguments. The way that you can combat their faulty logic is to present it with more Bible. The Bible is a book of answers. If you have questions about one part of the Bible, you can find the answers in another area. This is why it is essential to understand the Bible in its entirety. If you were the head coach of a football team, would you only focus on offense? No! You would lose the game quickly. Studying the Bible is the same way! You will be able to build a strong defense against your enemies and equip offensively to live a prosperous life!

Now we have seen the enemy's scheme, let's look into what he asks Jesus to do. Jesus was asked to jump off the highest part of the temple. Even though He would have been able to save Himself, Jesus could have gotten into a mess. The mess would have happened due to a lack of faith. If Jesus had thrown Himself down, it would signal that He was giving into the enemy's tricks and attempts to test God!

The enemy can't physically kill you. So, he will try to place you in a situation like Jesus to test our faith. God is in control, and you have to understand that He knows more than we do. As a student of Christ, it makes no sense to test our Teacher. The enemy wants you to throw yourself away, trying to be a daredevil. Whenever you are a daredevil, you always push yourself to the edge in life. Spiritually, this is dangerous! The enemy not only wants to push you to the edge, but he also wants to make you go over it! Stand firm in your faith and remember that daredevil always ends with evil!

3. Serve Him Only

So far, there are two ways the enemy attacked Jesus. First, the enemy tried to steal Jesus' appetite. Next, he tries to convince Jesus to kill Himself. The final way that the enemy attacks is seduction. There have been many instances in the Bible, where we have seen the enemy seduce people. Don't confuse seduction with just lust! The enemy attempts to seduce Jesus by taking him back to a "very high mountain." The mountain is symbolic of the high places in your life. Take a moment and think about your dream job. Is it the President of the United States? A CEO in Silicon Valley? Star quarterback in the NFL? Whatever that place is for you, imagine the enemy taking you there. At the high place, the enemy showed Jesus all of the riches that He could have. I'd imagine the enemy presented Jesus with a briefcase full of millions of dollars. Remember, Jesus was a carpenter! All the things that the enemy showed Jesus would've been foreign to a carpenter. If I handed you the briefcase, wouldn't you take it? Exactly, yes! All of those riches would have the potential not only to help you, but every generation after you!

The problem with seduction is that you become attracted to distractions. Isn't this what happened to Sampson? He became too focused on Delilah that it steered his focus away from saving Israel. Today, we see this with commercials. Whenever you are watching television, think about all the automobile commercials. The automaker's goal is to seduce you. All the new and improved features are shown during the thirty seconds. However, in the end, they briefly show the MSRP and leasing options. It always makes me laugh how little time these companies spend talking about the price. You would think that they would start with the price based on how much it cost! This is exactly what the enemy tries to do to us! Amid all the things presented to Jesus, look at what the enemy says. "All this I will give you," he said, "if you will bow down and worship me" (Matthew 4:9). How clever!

The one condition that the enemy presents to Jesus is enough to ruin the whole deal. Not like Jesus would have taken it anyway! Even though things presented in your life may look good, you must make sure that it is God. Don't just take things without understanding the terms and conditions. We started by talking about the enemy trying to steal your hunger, but he attempts to fill you with the wrong things like in this case. All the things that the enemy presented to Jesus would be satisfying, but only temporarily. Why? It would have lacked substance! Jesus understood that it would have steered him away from His purpose. Like Jesus, you must know that the enemy intends the same for you! Don't be driven away! Stay focused on your purpose!

In the final moments on the mountain, Jesus gives us a glimpse of how to defeat the enemy ultimately. Remember throwing stones is not enough; we must also cut off the head! Jesus said to him, *"Away from me, Satan!"* We must understand that we have the right to speak to our enemies because the spirit of Jesus lives in us. The Scripture says, "Resist the devil, and he will flee from you" (James 4:7). Whenever we are faced with attacks from the enemy, we must rebuke him! Jesus sets the enemy straight by telling him, "'Worship the Lord your God and serve him only'" (Matthew 4:10). We cannot sell our souls to the enemy in exchange for tangible things. Jesus turned down what was seen because God had so much in store for Him. Jesus starts and ends with Scripture!

This is how you ultimately win on the battlefields of life. Your faith is the stone, and the Word is your sword! Whenever the enemy feels like the "Goliath" in your life, you can defeat him. Use your faith to knock him down, and then God's Word will make the enemy flee! Remember, the battles in your life have a purpose. They are intended to make you stronger. There were a lot of things that both David and Jesus learned about themselves on their battlefields. God wants the same for you. To win on these battlefields, you must know how to fight. The fight for purpose is God's way of developing you. He has given you the stones to defeat your giants, but it is your responsibility to pick them up.

Thought: There are times in our life where we must fight for purpose. God has designed for the giants in our

life to mold and prepare us for where He has called for us
to be.

7

Started From the Bottom, Now We're Here

In Genesis 18, Sarah, Abraham's wife, is in a predicament. Sarah and Abraham have been trying to have children for decades. Sarah is almost ninety years old, so she gives up on the idea of having children. Suddenly, the Lord comes down to Earth to have a conversation with Abraham. God tells Abraham, "I will surely return to you about this time next year, and Sarah, your wife, will have a son" (Gen. 18:10). Sarah overhears the conversation and begins to laugh. Sarah laughs in disbelief. She believes that she is too old for her assignment. However, God sees it otherwise.

God hears Sarah's laugh and tells her that she shall have a child named Isaac, which means *"he laughs."* Sarah does indeed have a son the next year showing everything God spoke over her life did indeed come to pass. Now, why would Sarah laugh about something she waited so long for? Why would she laugh about the thing God was calling for her life? Sarah thought what God said was preposterous! A woman her age giving birth was completely unrealistic!

However, God had different plans for her life. He wanted to use Sarah to display His power to make a way out of no way. The same way, He uses Sarah is exactly how He can use you!

Like Sarah, we all have the same apprehension about our purpose. It may not be about being *"too old,"* but could be feeling *"not qualified"* or *"not smart enough"* for that job, person, or opportunity that God is calling for you in this season. What happens in our lives is like what happens in Sarah's life. Sarah went through years of failure. The moment she wants to give up is exactly when God comes and gives her the thing she has been waiting on. Her laughter was a result of her believing she was not qualified for her assignment. Sarah suffered from Imposter syndrome which is the notion of feeling unqualified. How many times has God positioned you somewhere that you have felt unqualified? We think that walking into God's mission for us will only expose our weaknesses. The enemy strategically wants us to focus on our deficiencies because it creates a sense of inadequacy. We focus so much on the shortcomings that we start to ignore God's assignment. Remember that God factored in all your deficiencies whenever He created you, and everything He has made He has plans to use!

Let's take a look to Luke 19 to one of my favorite stories in the Bible about a man named Zacchaeus. In this story, we see God using someone's weaknesses to activate purpose. Zacchaeus was a chief tax collector in Jericho and was very wealthy. Whenever Jesus passes through, crowds formed to see Him. Zacchaeus wants to see Jesus and attempts to look along with the crowd. His short stature hindered his ability to see Jesus with the crowd. Zacchaeus finds a sycamore-fig tree and climbs to the top of the tree. Jesus says, "Zacchaeus, come down immediately. I must stay at your house today." (Luke 19:5). All the people begin to mutter and gossip about Jesus entering the house, and Zacchaeus responds by giving his wealth away to the people he originally took it from.

There are a couple of takeaways from Zacchaeus' story to understand how God can use your weakness to propel you into purpose. The Bible shows that Zacchaeus' deficiency, his height, was the one thing that hindered his ability to find Jesus. Often, we are like Zacchaeus where weaknesses have made us feel as if we have come up short (pun not intended). It may not be with your height, but each of us have something that produces a sense of inadequacy. The inadequate feeling is essentially "lack of height" spiritually, where now your faith has come up short. Your deficiency has now affected your faith. You begin to dwell so much on your weaknesses that you begin to ignore your strengths.

What Zacchaeus realized was despite his shortcoming, he must persevere to see Jesus. Perseverance was how he got to be a wealthy tax collector! Tax collectors are known for never taking "no" as an answer. They will go to the ends of the Earth to collect people's debts. Many people despise tax collectors for their persistence, just as many Jews did with Zacchaeus. Now let's change the situation. Zacchaeus desired to find Jesus and knew that he would not be able to see over the crowd. However, he tapped into his strength of persistence. He refused to take no as an answer and was determined to find Jesus. Zacchaeus transferred his strengths from taking people's money to chasing after Jesus. Zacchaeus chose to use his strengths to overcome the limitations created by his weakness.

Your Disadvantage is Your Advantage

How many things in your life right now make you feel like Sarah and Zacchaeus? Are there moments that you feel like you have come up short in life? If the answer is yes, then you are in the right place. The Bible has a proven track record of using man's deficiencies to fulfill God's intended purpose, whether it be Noah's drunkenness of Moses' speech impediment. Therefore, whatever your weakness, God factored all of it in whenever He created you. Think about it. Zacchaeus' weaknesses led him to go up the tree. Whenever Zacchaeus reaches the top of the tree, he can see the same thing that everyone else sees; however, he now sees it on a higher level. He now experiences life on a higher level, both physically and spiritually. Yet, if Zacchaeus had never been limited by his height, he would have never thought about climbing the tree.

God used Zacchaeus' weakness as an opportunity to highlight His creativity. Zacchaeus' deficiency was the exact thing that forced him to think outside the box. God shows Zacchaeus that He will provide once Zacchaeus searches for the right thing - Jesus. This is the basis of Romans 8:28, when Paul says, "All things work together for the good of those who love The Lord, and are called according to His purpose." The qualifier in this verse is "according to His purpose" because if you are walking in the purpose of God, He will always make a way. God has a plan, even with your weaknesses. Just like a bow and arrow, God uses our shortcomings and weaknesses to hold us back until the right moment to propel us forward into our destiny.

Climb Your Tree

Let's dive deeper into the life of Zacchaeus. So we already know that Zacchaeus' height presented challenges for him to see Jesus over the crowds of people. It would have been easy for him to stop searching for Jesus. Zacchaeus could have just stayed in the crowd, frustrated with his dilemma. Whenever we focus too much on our weaknesses, we give up on achieving goals. We settle. We rely on the crowd's interpretation of Jesus.

What man sees as a weakness; God sees as an opportunity to display His power.

What "crowd" is blocking you from your purpose? Don't just see the "crowd" as your friends but you can also include family. Sometimes we settle for the crowd whenever we depend on our family's relationship with Jesus instead of forming our own. Sometimes, the crowd can even be your pastors or church leaders! Zacchaeus doesn't settle for the crowd! Zacchaeus had the mentality that he had to experience Jesus for himself, and so should you!

Stop relying solely on other people's experiences with Jesus to fix your problems. God is omnipresent, meaning that He can be everywhere all at once. God has made Himself available to you, but the question is will you seek Him? God wants you to begin to see how great you are! That greatness comes from overcoming your weaknesses. When Zacchaeus could not find any way to see Jesus, God provided a tree. Stop worrying about what is holding you back, and start looking for the tree God provided for you.

Have you felt like your weaknesses were causing you to not achieve the goals that you have planned? Do you feel like you have hit rock bottom in life because you always come up short? Well, I have good news. God is providing your tree. The tree is God's way of letting us know that He has the power to get us out of any situation.

Think about Moses in Exodus 14; God uses a tree in the form of staff to free the Israelites from Egypt. Go back to the story of Gideon. He was so worried about how to defeat the Midianites, but God placed the answer under a tree. Jesus dealt with a world stricken with sin and defiance, but the ultimate solution was Him dying on a tree. God has given us the power to see Jesus by climbing

---

Whenever you face adversity, God provides an opportunity.

---

our tree! It may not be climbing physically, but more so climbing spiritually. Climbing your tree spiritually means building a relationship with God. It is all about growth which means there must be a commitment to the sacrifice of climbing.

Everyone's tree looks different! Your relationship with God will allow you to understand where God is calling you to go. No one paid attention while Zacchaeus climbed his tree. Once he gets to the top, he sees the same Jesus but from a different perspective. Like Zacchaeus, God is waiting for you to get to your new level in life! God is looking to transform your life in all aspects. It's time for you to "level up" spiritually!

Leveling up spiritually allows you to reach new heights physically AND spiritually. People will begin to look at your life differently and be surprised by how God transforms it. I'd imagine people were so shocked seeing Zacchaeus at the top of that tree. Similarly, people will talk about you saying things like, *"How did he get THAT job"* or *"She makes HOW much!?!"* Their response is the result of you choosing to climb your tree.

Ready to dive deeper? Okay, let's go! What if I told you Jesus was waiting on Zacchaeus the whole time! As soon as Zacchaeus gets to the top of the tree, Jesus calls his name. The same man people despised, the same man that was too short to see, is the one that Jesus was looking for. Here is a hypothesis: what if Jesus served as a distraction to the crowd so that Zacchaeus could climb? Jesus wanted Zacchaeus to reach the next level before He speaks to Him. A spiritual distraction! What if God is doing the same thing in your life? God distracts certain people in your life so that you can be elevated. If you are worried that people don't notice you or ignore you because of your weaknesses, please stop worrying! God is distracting them so that you can grow. The same groups of people who counted you out in one season are the same people who will count on you once you climb your tree!

Come Down and Share the Fruit

What is Zacchaeus' reward for climbing his tree? Jesus says, "Zacchaeus, come down immediately. I must stay at your house today" (Luke 19:5).

Wait?

So, Zacchaeus has to go all the way up the tree, just for him to have to come down from the tree. Why would Jesus do such a thing? Could it be that if Zacchaeus stays in the tree, he would have gotten used to the level he was on? Zacchaeus probably would've been conceited and then would have forgotten the real reason he was in the tree in the first place.

The same thing happens in our lives. Spiritually, whenever we experience Jesus on a different level, we can often forget where we came from. Even in church, we see people judging others but forget about the life they lived before finding God. Jesus wants you to come down from your tree to humble us and get us back down to Earth. God lets you experience everything on a different level, but His intention is not for you to become complacent. God wants you to get down from the tree, but now with a changed mindset. You will now tell the people about the same Jesus but from a new and fresh perspective.

However, please understand that as you come down, people will still gossip about you. Don't worry about what people have to say! The crowd began to mutter about Jesus, saying, "He has gone to be the guest of a sinner." Showing that people will always speak on the person you used to be, but God speaks on the person you will become! Zacchaeus comes down and repays the people he used to take money from as a tax collector. Zacchaeus exemplifies what Paul says in 2 Corinthians 5:17, "Therefore, if anyone is in Christ, the new creation has come: The old has gone, the new is here!"

Before the tree, Zacchaeus takes money from people but once he comes down from the tree, he gives it away. See the mindset shift? God didn't provide the tree to change Zacchaeus' position, but He wanted to change the posture of Zacchaeus' heart. The same is true for our tree. Trees naturally are meant to give! Whether the tree provides shade on a hot day or the paper that this book is printed on, trees give a lot to us. The tree is a symbol of what God intends for humanity. Once we adjust our posture to share God's blessings with others, then we please Him the way Zacchaeus does at the end of this story.

There are times where the things God is calling for us to do simply just make us laugh like Sarah or forces us out of our comfort zones like Zacchaeus. God has strategically called you for something greater. What God is asking for you to do may seem impossible, but He wants you to understand that all things are possible through Him. Philippians 4:13 states, "I can do ALL things through Christ who strengthens me." Meaning that God can still allow me to give birth to something special despite the way my situation looks. Let's look at a modern-day example.

Award-winning author Nick Vujicic has been to multiple countries, motivating millions of people. Through schools, orphanages, hospitals, and other areas, Nick uses his gifts to inspire generations through his testimony. Due to a rare disease called Tetra-Amelia Syndrome, Nick was born without arms and legs. In his story, Nick describes battling with depression and loneliness during his childhood; but he was determined not to let his lack of limbs forfeit his purpose in life. God had a plan in Nick's life, and his story encapsulates everything in making your disadvantage your advantage.

Many people in the world are motivational speakers that have engagements around the globe. However, Nick's story made him different. God used what man saw as his weakness as an opportunity to use him to inspire millions of people around the world. I believe people are more susceptible to being motivated by Nick Vujicic's story because if he can find purpose in life, we can too! Nick is now President and CEO of his own nonprofit, Life Without Limbs, and uses his life as an example of God's chosen vessel. In the same way that God is using Nick, He has special plans for your life as well.

The plans for your life have already been ordained. Your calling is waiting for you! In the midst of your shortcomings, God still sees you as His own. Jeremiah 29:11 states, "For I know the plans that I have for you"- showing that God has planned out your life before you even took your first breath. Stop looking at your weaknesses as a burden and start to look at them as a blessing. When you shift your perspective, you will realize all the opportunities that God has in front of you, and you will then be prepared to be launched into your destiny. Leadership is all about growth. Tony Robbins sums up leadership like this, *"If you're not growing, you're dying."* Growth looks different for everyone. Maybe it might be professionally with jobs and promotions. If that's not you right now, perhaps it might be building the relationships in your life.

These are three ways to help you overcome your weaknesses.

1. Identify Your Weakness

One of the most popular questions in any type of interview is, *"What are your strengths and weaknesses?"* The question is so important because your answer affects the organization's culture and potentially its productivity. This is why these questions usually are at the beginning of the interview. Often, when discussing our weakness, we say something generic to appease our audience. Our answers probably consist of something along the lines of, "*I have trouble saying no*" or "*I am impatient.*" Even though you may get the job or position, your real strengths and weaknesses will always expose themselves in due time. You must often interview yourself. Don't answer with the politically correct answer! You must be honest with yourself. The vital part of knowing yourself is understanding your weaknesses. Everyone has weaknesses. Zacchaeus knew that he was short. He didn't sulk about it. He embraced it! Paul expresses that he boasts about his weaknesses so that Christ's power may rest on him. Understand where you are weak and what your limitations are. The first step in overcoming your weakness is accepting it. Once you accept your weakness, then you can begin the steps towards dealing with it.

2. Focus on your Strengths

One of my favorite quotes is from a book called *Help! I Work With People*, by Pastor Chad Veach. He says, "*Denying what you're good at isn't humility, it's just denial.*" Don't deny your strengths. It's essential you distinguish between boasting and focusing. There is a difference between letting everyone know how good you are at something versus being so good at something that everyone knows. When I watch the NBA playoffs, one of the teams that have been interesting to watch is the Brooklyn Nets. In the middle of the season, the general manager decided to trade critical players and embrace their offensive abilities. The moves shifted the NBA and have revolutionized the game of basketball.

What makes the Nets' strategy attractive is that they base every decision on analytics. The data suggest that 3-pointers are better than 2-pointers. So what did they do? They brought more 3-point shooters on the team. You can see their commitment to the three-point shot every time you see them play. They even give up wide-open layups for a 3-point shot. They understand as a team that their strength is shooting 3-pointers, and they focus on it. Win or lose, they have committed to that play style because they have zoned in on their strengths. The Nets give us a lesson on how we should live. Find your 3-point shot. What separates you from others? What makes you unique? Whatever that may be in your life, find it, and focus on it.

3. Lead By Example

Zacchaeus doesn't just talk, but he also walks the walk. Whenever Jesus calls him off of the tree, Zacchaeus tells everyone that he would pay the poor and repay anyone he had "defrauded" (Luke 19:8). The important thing to note is that he says this after people were gossiping about him. People said that Jesus had "gone to be the guest of a man who is a sinner."

Despite everyone having their opinion on Zacchaeus, he chose to take the higher road. There will be many different occasions in life where people will have things to say about the person you were. People will talk about you, and they may be right but take the higher road. Zacchaeus answered the common question that everyone asks today, "*What would Jesus do?*" Look at Jesus' response to Zacchaeus. He says, "Today salvation has come to this house, because he, too, is a son of Abraham."

What a powerful statement! Jesus shows us that salvation changed Zacchaeus' heart. The same way that Zacchaeus leads by example, so can you. Amid adversity, Zacchaeus didn't change heart. Neither should we! Michelle Obama says, "*When they go low, we go high.*" Be the example. Don't worry about what others say. Focus on what Jesus would do. Let me reiterate. Paul writes it best in 2 Corinthians. He says, "... I will boast all the more gladly about my weaknesses, so that Christ's power may rest on me." Your weak-

> There is a difference between letting everyone know how good you are at something versus being so good at something that everyone knows.

nesses are necessary because they can help you activate your purpose. Don't let your shortcoming or limitations hold you back because they are the very thing that God is setting up to propel you forward.

* * *

What's the Big Idea?

There are many occupations that Jesus has: priest, prophet, king. However, there is another occupation that we often don't associate with Jesus, a carpenter. When Jesus and His disciples went back to His hometown, one of the first questions that they asked was, "Isn't this the carpenter?" (Mark 6:3). When you imagine a carpenter, what picture comes to mind? I picture a man with a toolbelt and a lunchbox trying to fix a table. Certainly not an executive on Wall Street or a software engineer in Silicon Valley. In today's world, carpenter might be considered a low-level job. My favorite movie is Spike Lee's, *Malcolm X*. As a kid, Malcolm was one of the top students in his class. Despite being a scholar, whenever the students discussed their career paths, the teacher suggested that Malcolm should be a carpenter. The teacher believed Malcolm could only be a carpenter because that was one of the only accepted "black" occupations. His teacher believed that carpentry was a common job. In ancient Palestine, carpentry, too, was also considered a job for the common people. No wonder people were so perplexed that a carpenter was revolutionizing the world with His ministry!

When observing the life of Jesus, we see the impact of His effectiveness in leadership. We see His large number of followers along with the many people who were healed. Most of His ministry tied back to His knowledge of carpentry. We discussed how weakness can help launch you into your purpose. Since Jesus had no weakness, there are lessons that we can learn from Him about how He took a "low-level" job as a carpenter and used that to activate His purpose.

1. Know Your Toolbelt

Before you begin to build anything, you must first learn to use your tools. Carpenters can't repair a table without knowing how to use a hammer. Before Jesus started any public ministry, we saw Him at twelve years old in a temple. Often, we dwell on the fact that Mary and Joseph lost Jesus. However, I believe from an alternate perspective, Jesus learned an important lesson with His development as a leader. Jesus understood that before you begin to build you must first know your toolbelt. In this case, I am not talking about a typical wrench or a drill. I am referring to your spiritual tool belt. Your spiritual toolbelt refers to all the gifts that God has given for you to live out your purpose. The Apostle Paul outlines these gifts of the Holy Spirit in 1 Corinthians 12:

"The Holy Spirit is given to each of us in a special way. That is for the good of all. To some people the Spirit gives a message of wisdom. To others the same Spirit gives a message of knowledge. To others the same Spirit gives faith. To others that one Spirit gives gifts of healing. To others he gives the power to do miracles. To others he gives the ability to prophesy. To others he gives the ability to tell the spirits apart. To others he gives the ability to speak in different kinds of languages they had not known before. And to still others he gives the ability to explain what was said in those languages. All the gifts are produced by one and the same Spirit. He gives gifts to each person, just as he decides" (1 Corinthians 12:7-11).

Can you identify your gifts? There are many gifts, but don't miss two crucial words that Paul says, "to some." Notice he doesn't say "to all" or "everybody." Everyone has access to the same Holy Spirit through Jesus Christ, but it does not mean that we have all of the gifts. God is strategic! He has given each of us different gifts, skills, and abilities so that we can function as a true body of Christ. The important thing with you in the body of Christ is that you must know the gifts you have before you begin to learn how to use those gifts.

Jesus in the temple was completely aware of His assignment on Earth. However, I believed that as both God and man, the flesh of Jesus had to understand how to navigate with others including His own family. See, what we must realize is that leadership requires pace. Yes, Jesus impressed the people in the temple with His knowledge and His abilities. However, what I believe that Jesus recognizes is that His focus caused Him to miss His own family. I believe that twelve-year-old Jesus wasn't quite aware yet of the impact of His toolbelt. Mary recognizes the power of Jesus and knew that it was not time for it to be used. How do we know? In the next verse, it says, "Then he went down to Nazareth with them and was obedient to them" (Luke 2:51). Why was Jesus obedient? He is cognizant of the fact that there was still learning to be done. There was more He needed to know about His toolbelt.

Jesus was not wrong for wanting to be in the temple, listening, and asking questions. Twelve-year-old Jesus probably would've spent most of His time questioning the teachers of the law if He had not been obedient to His parents. Jesus would've been impressive, but would He have been as effective? A lot of times we face this own issue in our lives. We feel comfortable in environments where we can impress people, instead of being obedient to our Father and going to where we will be effective. As a response to Jesus' obedience, He "grew in wisdom and stature" (v. 52). Notice it didn't say grow in knowledge. Jesus is truth wrapped in flesh! Wisdom refers to the ability to use that truth effectively. The wisdom that Jesus gains is necessary for you to learn as you continue to grow in Christ. Yes, you know the tools you have. That's not it! You must also know how to use them and when to use your tools. Even though it will be impressive to some, God is preparing you for the season where you will be effective to many.

2. Jack of All Trades

In the Bible, Jesus: cast out demons, heals a paralyzed man, feeds five thousand, heals a leper, and even raises a man from the dead. Just to name a few! There are so many titles that we can classify with Jesus. In the handyman world, Jesus is known as a "jack-of-all-trades." This refers to a person who can perform different types of work. Who knew a carpenter had that kind of power! The important thing to note is that Jesus' ministry was not limited to one specific thing. Today, culture defines this concept as a "side hustle." We see many posts telling us that the key to wealth is having multiple streams of income. Conversely, the church goes away from this and makes you believe that ministers can only focus on one thing.

Your ministry is unique! Jesus had many titles: carpenter, teacher, pastor, prophet, doctor, and even entrepreneur. Yes! Jesus was the most famous entrepreneur in history. Despite His many titles, Jesus preached the same message regardless of His occupation. In the same way, don't let your labels limit you from ministering to people. One of my mentors is the CEO of his own company and continues to minister to me daily! You have the ability to have a number of occupations and still minister to people! Don't let people make you think that ministry is one lane. If it was only one lane, then it wouldn't be able to reach around the world! Wherever you are, whatever job you may have, you can still minister to people.

Since ministry is unique, it looks different for everyone. That just means that there is a special group of people that need your ministry. From the boardroom, the basketball court, or just in your home you can minister just like Jesus. What you must realize is this secret...Jesus didn't need a title to validate His ministry. He didn't need anyone putting the words "pastor" or "apostle" before He spoke. It is not about the title; it is about the anointing. Just because you might have not gone down the traditional route doesn't mean that you can't minister to people. Being a "jack-of-all-trades" comes more from experience than education. Your life experience becomes valuable with your ministry. Let this encourage you...Jesus wasn't traditional! You were made to stand out! You have the ability to chase your dreams and still minister to people along the way!

3. Build by Faith

Jesus applies His carpentry knowledge to His ministry in many ways. One way, in particular, stands out the most in Matthew 16 where Jesus is speaking with His disciples. In a series of questions, Jesus inquires about how people view Him. Jesus then asks His own disciples, "Who do you say I am?" (Matthew 16:15). Peter answers, "You are the Messiah, the Son of the living God" (v.16). There are many lessons that we can take from Peter's response; however, look at Jesus' response to Peter's confession. Jesus says, "And I tell you that you are Peter, and on this rock I will build my church, and the gates of Hades will not overcome it" (Matthew 16:18).

There is no coincidence that Jesus chose to paint the scene as a carpenter. Look at the words that He uses *"rock," "build,"* and *"gates"*

Jesus didn't need a title to validate His ministry.

---

are all words that a true carpenter would use. Jesus uses these words in order to give Peter tangible insight about the reward for his faith. Peter's faith is the cornerstone for the church as we know it today. Newsflash! Jesus still intends for the church to be built today. You indeed are a carpenter! Jesus wants to continue to build through you. Think about what you are building in this season. This can range from a business to a family. Like Peter, it can only be built based on the confession of your faith. Jesus models faith as a rock because our faith must be solid. In life, there will be many tests and obstacles that you will be forced to overcome. The only thing that keeps you focused in the face of adversity is your faith.

Do you have faith? It is important that you understand this before you build anything. If you are not led by faith, then as soon as you are presented with an obstacle you will immediately jump ship. See, what you must know is that praying and having faith are two different things. Whenever Jesus asks the disciples about His Divine nature, He doesn't say, *"Peter, who do you say I am?"* He asked all of the disciples, but only Peter spoke up and answered. The problem wasn't that Peter was a teacher's pet or that person that tries to answer every question. The difference between Peter and the rest of the disciples was his faith. Peter not only speaks up, but in another instance, he responds to Jesus' call by stepping out of a boat and walking on water (Matthew 14:22). This is why I believe Jesus admires Peter's faith because not only did he confess his faith, but he showed it through his actions.

Wherever you want to go in life, you must have faith. In order to activate your purpose, you must have faith in Jesus. Did you see the difference? Anybody can have faith in worldly things and reach a goal. Having faith in Jesus not only helps you reach your goals but exceeds your goals. If Peter would have had simply just had faith, he would've gotten a couple more fish each day. However, once Peter placed his faith in Jesus, he was able to do the supernatural. In your life, Jesus wants to do the supernatural! In your mind, I know you have dreams about every aspect of your life. For every carpenter, the stage before the building is dreaming. Every builder envisions what they are building beforehand and works towards those goals.

For you, it could simply be building your vocabulary or building your Instagram presence. Let Jesus take control, and He will amaze you with the results. Whenever you allow Jesus to take control, He will raise you from the bottom and into your destiny. In the last section, we talked about your spiritual tool belt. You must realize you don't have all the tools! The good news is that your faith allows you to pass the blueprint to the One who has all the tools!

Thought: God created everything about you, even your weaknesses, for His unique purpose. Don't let your weakness be the thing that holds you back from your calling, instead embrace it and let it be the thing that launches you into purpose.

8

Blessed Through A Mess

Have you ever been in a messy situation wondering why God would allow your life to get this way? The bills are due, your marriage is simply not working, and your job is talking about layoffs. The thought becomes: *"How can a God of love make me suffer so much?"* Everything is always going right and then BOOM! Here comes a bunch of unexpected circumstances. It's time for you to know that you are not alone in your suffering. The reality of life is that suffering is inevitable. Even in the Bible, one of the most prevalent themes is suffering. David had to suffer. Joseph had to suffer. Even Jesus had to suffer.

Many times we can get ourselves in messy situations. However, what hurts the most is when it seems as if you have done everything right, but suffering still comes. Like me, you've probably had that moment in school where you study all night for that exam, and you still fail. Or you have tried everything you can for a relationship, but things are just not working. Situations like these are when life gets frustrating. We start to feel like the Israelites when they tell Moses, "Was it because there were no graves in Egypt that you brought us to the desert to die? What have you done to us by bringing us out of Egypt?" (Exodus 14:11) The Israelites could have gone the easy way, but God chose to take them a long way. Sometimes it feels like God makes us go the "long way" for no reason. However, God uses the "long way" to teach us things along the way.

There were many lessons that the Israelites learned in the wilderness, one of them being the Ten Commandments! By the time they arrive at the Promised Land, a new generation enters. The new generation isn't just about the children of Israel, it is about a fresh mindset. God wants the same things for your life. Oftentimes, God takes us through messy situations in order to force us to grow. God has already lined up the promises for your life, but He wants your mindset to change so that you can grasp all that He has to offer.

Here's a different example. If we were to tell people that they had one wish, most people's wishes would probably center around finance. Whether it be unexpected income or a promotion career-wise. These things all center around the same thing, money. So let's say we ask God for one million dollars. There are many ways that God could bless us with money. Our hopes would probably be that we wake up one morning and our checking account reads $1,000,000 dollars. Then we would probably praise God, run around our house, and kiss everyone in sight. It is more than likely that our next action would be spending. We would get the newest sneakers, pay off any immediate bills, and maybe go get that new car that has been sitting at the dealership. Do you see the problem? The focus with the money has been around one person, you.

Now let's look at another scenario. Let's say that we have prayed to God for the million dollars. For years, you endured seasons of living paycheck to paycheck. However, you learn how to save your money. You cut on your spending and become financially literate. After years of praying, saving, and investing, you look up one morning, and you look at all of your assets which are valued at

---

God uses the "long way" to teach us things along the way.

$1,000,000 dollars. You feel accomplished. You still thank God for the money but also you are appreciative of the increase in wisdom. Both situations result in blessings. God not only wanted to give you the blessing but can you sustain the blessing? Don't lose hope whenever your situation looks messy. Maybe God is trying to teach you something.

God uses time to test the faith of His chosen people, He wants you to understand the power within you! This is why God takes Moses through the Red Sea to show him the power of the staff in his hands. Sometimes you can only recognize that power through a messy situation. When it feels like your back is against the wall, that is when you are the most creative. This is no coincidence! Many celebrities in the world today first had humble beginnings. God uses people's unfortunate situations to perform miracles. Then there's no question that He deserves the glory. We often get caught up in receiving blessings, when instead, we should thank God for getting us out of a mess.

Take a deeper look into everyone's favorite holiday, Christmas. Today, the story of Christmas is all about gifts and family. However, Christmas is about suffering. Generation after generation, we have obsessed over endless commercials with the newest toys, devices, and other shiny new things. In all of this, we miss the meaning of Christmas. Jesus is the WHY of Christmas, but I want to focus on the HOW of Christmas. We understand that Jesus was born, but what did it take for Him to be born? To understand the HOW of Jesus' birth we have to analyze His mother, Mary.

For Mary, everything happened suddenly when God sent forth His Son. Mary was pledged to be married to Joseph. She probably had the wedding already planned out. Then the angel, Gabriel, shares the news that God will bless her with the birth of Jesus. The news shakes up Mary's entire world. What is she going to tell Joseph? As soon as she is ready to get married, God shakes up her world. Have you ever been so comfortable with life then it feels like everything is breaking loose? Are there times where you feel exactly like Mary? Everything seems to be going to plan, then something comes up that shifts everything. Sometimes God has to force us to get uncomfortable so that you can fulfill His purpose in your life.

Think back to Jonah. God had to create a storm in Jonah's life in order to align with His intended purpose. The storms in your life may just be God's detour to get you in the right direction. God shakes things up in Moses' life by calling him down from the mountain to go save the Israelites. Whenever things are being shaken up in your life, don't worry, just know that God is up to something special! So, when God calls Mary to give birth, things start to get messy. People around her probably saw she was pregnant and believed she was an adulterer. People were probably gossiping behind her back. There were probably questions circulating like *"Who was Mary sleeping with?"* or *"Is this even Joseph's baby?"* Understand that whenever God activates purpose, people will make assumptions about you. There will be people talking about you! Gossip is one of the enemy's strategies to distract you from purpose. People always will talk whenever they begin to see you change. You have got to understand that the enemy does not want to see you change. The enemy realized what Mary had inside of her. Jesus' potential impact is the reason why the enemy tried to make things hard for Mary! The same enemy sees your power and is trying to do whatever to stop you before you realize it.

Blessed Through a Mess

The first lesson that we can learn from Mary's life is this: God's timing is NOT aligned with our timing. Mary anticipated marrying Joseph. She probably did expect to have kids, but she was not expecting it to happen in that manner. God called her to be the exception! The examples given through Mary's life is the reason why you can't live your life based on what society says. Your life looks different than everyone else's! That's okay. God is also calling you to be the exception! There are many times that God calls exceptions. No one expected a young shepherd to defeat Goliath or a murderer to be the one that God calls to be His apostle. In almost every person's life, the call from God is never expected. Maybe you're not fighting any giants anytime soon or traveling around the world to preach, but God has called everyone to give birth to something special.

The beautiful thing about God is that everything that He says will come to pass. The angel tells Mary, "For no word from God will ever fail." (Luke 1:37) So the calling over your life is not dependent on your current situation. God has created that situation for a specific reason. He intends to teach you things through that situation to give you a new perspective of Him. The reality is that your situation is a blessing in itself. In your life, there will be people who will only relate to your situation. Paul's ministry was so unique because he was able to speak to everyone. His previous life as Saul was very messy. However, God knew that Paul would have to go and minister to people who had the same background. So in the midst of his sin, God still had purpose.

Stop letting your messes hinder your ability to walk into your purpose. The mess has meaning and sometimes in order to find your purpose it requires you to get messy. There was purpose found through many messes in the Bible! The trials and tribulations are simply meant to strengthen you. In Genesis, Joseph tells his brothers once they reunite, "You meant evil against me, but God used it for good." (Genesis 50:20) So the very mess that the enemy is trying to keep you in, God will turn that situation around and bless you through it.

Stop Stressing Over Your Blessing

Your immediate response after reading the last section was probably, *"Yeah that sounds good and all but... I still need help."* Well, then, let's continue with the story of Mary. The whole town probably ostracized her at this point because she would've been seen as an infidel. I can imagine Mary just being stressed out and in need of assistance. She was in dire need of a miracle! So what did God do? He provides her with Joseph.

Even though they were pledged to be married, once Joseph saw that Mary was pregnant, he was determined to get a divorce. Joseph had to be angry! The woman that he was pledged to marry was pregnant and he was supposed to take care of the child? C'mon. During Joseph's frustration, God sent an angel to explain to him how the child was conceived. God's revelation helps Joseph take Mary as his wife and do what the Lord commanded.

There are many times where we feel as if we have to get through messes in life ourselves. We feel as if God is making us endure the hardships alone. That is not true! Remember, God loves and values relationships! He will send someone to help you through situations. Since Mary obeyed the Lord, then God began to work everything out for her. Any situation that God has called you into, He will always provide the right resources and people for you. God does the same thing by providing Elijah with food from the raven. He even helped Moses by providing him with Aaron to help him speak to Pharaoh. Whenever your needs are aligned with God's needs, that's exactly where miracles occur. God knew that Mary needed Joseph to help protect her from the townspeople. The townspeople would have disgraced her for being an adulteress. Even amid adversity, God still provided for her.

As the news of the baby Jesus began to develop, Caesar Augustus issued a decree for every man to return to his hometown. Which forced Joseph to take Mary with him to Bethlehem. The good news for Mary is that the sudden exit was helpful because Herod wanted to kill Jesus as we will talk about more later in the book. The enemy probably thought that Mary having to move to Bethlehem was a burden, but it in fact was simply a blessing of protection.

So God not only provides Mary with Joseph, but He also protects her through extraction. God will remove you from certain situations on purpose to protect you. There are a lot of times in our life where we get so caught up in the things around us. For Mary, it was the danger of being publicly disgraced. We might fear the same thing. It might not be to the extreme of being shunned like Mary, but it might be getting "canceled" on social media or disowned by the people you love because you follow God's commands.

Stop stressing!

The stress is distracting you from your blessing. Mary has Jesus inside of her. Jesus! The most important person to walk on the face of the Earth was inside of Mary! The situation on the outside looked messy. Society against her...Joseph probably passive-aggressive towards her... she is even forced to leave her own town to go all the way to Bethlehem. There are a lot of variables that probably would've caused us to stress out. God sees all of the variables that you have to deal with daily. He wants you to understand that He can get you out of your mess. He will help you overcome whatever situation you may be dealing with. Through God, you will receive the peace that surpasses all understanding that will turn your stress into rest.

Rest in Your Blessing

Mary travels with Joseph to Bethlehem. Mary is ready to give birth and they are searching for a place to deliver Jesus. They could not find a guest room, so they had to deliver the baby in a manger. Wait... so, the Prince of Peace, the Messiah, Immanuel is being delivered in the place where animals eat? So Mary left one messy situation only for it to be replaced with a literal mess in a manger. How fitting. Once again, Mary is in a messy place and that is exactly where God intends for her to be. We must remember this one phrase: God can bless through a mess. Maybe you didn't start out in a mess, but ended up in one. Mary shows us that God can still give birth to something special, even in a mess.

Let's think about it from this angle. In one season, Mary was in danger of being publicly disgraced because of her situation. People were going to drive her out of town, call her names, and shame her for what was inside of her. However, in the next season, people come to the manger to find Jesus. Understand that there are people who will try to drive you away in one season, but there are different people who will travel around the world to experience the gift inside of you.

There are, however, people who do not value what is inside of you. Mary's own people were going to be the same ones that publicly disgraced her simply because they didn't realize her purpose. Don't be discouraged that certain people leave you in one season, because God will position the right people to come find you. Trusting in God is also about trusting in the relationships that He gives you and takes away. There has to be a trust that God will provide the right people at the right time in your life.

The Mess Is Protection

God can bless through a mess.

Even if you are currently in a mess, you can still give birth to something. That business, that new job, or even that book can be started in the mess. In fact, the mess makes it that much more special. Think about it. Mary gives birth in the manger and only the shepherd and the wise men know where Jesus is born. Being in a manger works out for Mary whenever Herod is attempting to kill every baby while searching for Jesus. Sometimes, God waits until a messy situation happens before He brings something new to your life. The mess can serve as a distraction to people wanting to kill your purpose. People will be like, *"There's no way you can start that company she just got fired from her last job."* Based on where you currently are, they might be right, the odds may not look to be in your favor. Don't worry, that is exactly where God wants you!

The manger serves as temporary protection for Mary. See, if Mary would have given birth to Jesus at a fancy inn or one of the guesthouses, then people would have been able to know where Jesus was and report Him to Herod. There are some blessings in your life that aren't meant for everyone to see. The news of Jesus' birth would have immediately been "passed through the grapevine" to the Roman soldiers. Herod represents the people in this world that are willing to kill what is inside of you simply based on what they have heard. So, there are times where God places you in situations not to harm you but to protect you.

What about David? God protected David while he escaped from Saul. David was in a messy situation. Saul couldn't find David. He was looking to kill David because he was afraid of David's anointing. Saul went from town to town searching to find David. Through his mess, David relied on the Lord for assistance. Saul lost his own sons and died while David was still in hiding. There is purpose in everything. Both David and Mary had to leave normal and trust in God. Through the mess, David became king and Mary gave birth to a king. God is positioning you to give birth to something in your messy season. There are opportunities with your name on them, but it requires you to go through a mess!

God wants to bless you through your mess. There are many times where we are unsure of how to navigate through the messes in our life. The mess can be created by our decision making or it can be things outside of our control. Regardless, God will use your mess to make you stronger. Throughout the chapter, we have analyzed how to embrace and steer through the messes of life. I want to give you some tips about how to get rid of your mess. Don't be naïve and stay in your mess! You can strategically get out of the messes and live a more complete life.

In order to illustrate how to get out of your mess, I want to use an analogy to a cleanser that everyone is familiar with, Windex. Many of us have a strong relationship with Windex after years of completing daily chores. I know you are sitting here asking yourself, *"How does Windex relate to my life's issues?"*

1. Don't Ignore Your Chores

Growing up, my parents gave me a schedule of my daily chores. The chores would range from vacuuming the house to taking out the trash. My chores had to be done before school. Therefore, I had to wake up earlier in order to make sure that I was able to accomplish everything and get my mind ready for the school day. From my perspective, I wanted to get the chores finished so that I could avoid the consequences of not getting them done. However, my parents emphasized the importance of getting the chores done in a timely manner so that they wouldn't come home to a dirty house.

Both of us had our reasons for doing chores. We both understood that in order to keep the house in order the chores must be done.

Just like our physical house, it is necessary that we keep our spiritual house in order. Our temple is kept in order by doing our chores. Naturally, we call these moments "self-care days" where we flood spas and watch our favorite shows in order to alleviate stress. Why don't we have the same mindset with our spirit? If we neglect our spiritual chores, then we start to feel dirty. Why? The enemy will use distractions in the world to make you oblivious to these "dirty" spirits that he is using to make your life messy.

How do you combat this? Do your chores. Good news. God has given all of us our "Windex." Think about it. God made us to reflect His image. In a sense, we are like a mirror. When people look at us, they are supposed to see God through us. What dirties our mirrors? Sin. The enemy uses sin to turn us away from God. Our image gets dirty and it's hard to clearly reflect God. Understand, it is our fault, not God's. The good news is that God sent us a cleanser to get rid of our dirt. His name is Jesus Christ. Through Jesus, He cleanses all the dirt so that our images can become clear.

Once you clean your mirror one time, it doesn't mean that you never have to clean your mirror again. Since we all "sin and come short of the glory of God" (Romans 3:23), we must constantly cleanse our mirrors. We do this through repentance. Having a contrite heart through prayer, allows you to see the places that you are "dirty." Once you know where you are dirty, you can begin to ask God specifically where you need help. God will begin to cleanse your mess.

Don't ignore this!

There are many of us that forget prayer in a mess. Ignoring prayer is just like ignoring chores. There are consequences! Understand, none of us are perfect. However, if we incorporate these "spiritual" chores into our daily lives, then we will have Jesus and He will guide us to perfection.

2. Wipe the Mess

To use Windex effectively, there is one more thing that you need while cleaning. Can you guess? A paper towel. Maybe you don't necessarily use a paper towel. It could be a dish rag or if you are bougie then maybe it's one of those expensive washcloths from Bed Bath & Beyond. Ha! That's beside the point. To effectively clean any surface, you have to wipe it off. The point is that you must put in the work to clean anything. Wiping any surface ensures that the surface will be clean.

Spiritually, the same thing must happen for us to get cleansed. In the last section, we discussed how Jesus is our cleanser. Jesus can cleanse any situation regardless of how messy it may be. However, like we discussed earlier faith WITHOUT works is dead. You must understand this! If you put in the work, God will begin to work on your behalf. Once you choose Jesus, then you have to trust in Him to begin to work through your mess. God wants to use your mess to teach you, but you must be willing to put in the work to learn. Look at David's mess.

David was in a mess. He murders his friend just so he can take his wife. Talk about messy! It sounds like a reality TV show. Drama. Adultery. Murder. After talking with the prophet Nathan, David instantly repents. He says to Nathan, "I have sinned against the LORD" (2 Samuel 12:13). Look at what David does next! The Bible says that David "fasted and spent the nights lying in sackcloth on the ground." What can we learn? Even though David puts himself into a mess, he works to get himself out. Like David, we must work to get out of our mess by focusing on God about how to get through our situations. David wiped his mess and God blessed him with

Solomon. God wants to help you navigate through your mess. In order to get through your situation, you must be willing to take the steps to get rid of the mess. You are a significant part of the equation towards transformation. Wiping your mess can be studying the Bible more, fasting, and praying. Do the work and you will begin to wipe away your mess!

3. Avoid the Mess

The proverbial statement that has followed me from my childhood into adulthood is, "Work smarter, not harder!" Being forced to do chores at home, I quickly realized the importance of this statement. Each day, I woke up to complete my daily chores. As the weeks went by, I performed the chores over and over again. Then I had a sudden epiphany: most of the messes were my fault. In order to combat this, I had to change my lifestyle. If I could be more cognizant of my actions, the fewer chores I would have to do every day. Instead of using metal forks, I chose to eat with plastic forks. In order to minimize having to clean the mirrors weekly, I stayed away from always looking in the mirror while brushing my teeth. These small changes made a noticeable difference in my chores. I went from having to clean the mirror weekly to bi-weekly. As a result, I could use the time for other things. I could spend more time finishing homework, well more so watch ESPN. Ha!

For this to happen, I had to find ways to avoid the mess. This concept is not only applicable physically but also spiritually. The cycle that we have adopted today is: pray, repent, then repeat. Is this you? Prayer and repentance are not the issues, it is the repetition of sin. How many times have you committed a sin that you could not seem to break? Repeatedly, you are stuck trying to figure out what is wrong with you. The issue is not you; it is your environment. Let me put it this way. On your way to work or school every morning, there are probably many ways to get to your destination. For people that live in bigger cities, the main routes are usually clogged with traffic. Day after day, you sit in traffic wondering why there is traffic every day! In order to get to work on time, what do you do? Avoid the mess. You probably look on Google Maps or Waze to identify any back roads. This way you can wake up at the same time and not have to worry about the daily traffic.

Spiritually, sin is our traffic. It is the very thing that blocks you from God's purpose for your life. On the course of life, you cannot afford to spend seasons stuck in traffic. Spiritually, you must take steps to avoid the messes of life. How do you do that? Simple. Start by taking an inventory of the sins that you find yourself stuck to. Next, backtrack and think about what led you to that sin. Then, analyze how you can change your methods to help you avoid that sin.

I'll give you a personal example. One of the issues that I dealt with is pornography. For years, I was addicted to watching porn. I would happily watch porn but feel terrible afterward. Feeling ashamed, I would ask myself questions like, *"Why did you just do that?"* There came a day where I looked in the mirror and began the journey towards cleansing my mind of porn. One of the things that I noticed was that there was a common theme each time I would watch porn. It would always be nighttime, and I would always be alone. In order to deal with these issues, I started by changing those two variables.

Naturally, I am an introvert. Therefore, in order to solve my porn issue, I had to force myself to be more social. This forced me to step outside my comfort zone and meet more people. As a result, I became more focused on hanging out with my friends instead of watching porn. Being able to surround myself with Christ-centered friends was an additional plus. I was able to explain to them my situation and to my surprise, many of them dealt with the same issues. We not only hung out, but they also encouraged me while I took the necessary steps to overcome my addiction.

The important thing to remember is following Christ allows you to avoid the messes of life. Whatever "messy" situation you may be going through in life, hand it to God. You will see that God not only has the power to get you through but also bless you through the mess.

* * *

What's the Big Idea?

Jesus is with us in our mess. There are many stories that we can pull from to show how Jesus protects us, but there's one in particular that embodies how much Jesus cares about us. Jesus was with us since Creation. Even though we see the physical manifestation of Jesus in the New Testament, He was also with us in the Old Testament. The pre-manifestation of Jesus is what is known as a "Christophany." A Christophany is the pre-manifestation of Jesus in the Old Testament before He arrives in the New Testament. Some of the more well-known Christophanies were Melchizedek and the angel who wrestles with Jacob.

The Christophany that I want to focus on appears in the book of Daniel. Three Hebrew boys (Shadrach, Meshach, and Abednego) were the friends of the prophet Daniel who were sent into exile in Babylon. King Nebuchadnezzar appointed the three men as administrators over the province of Babylon at the request of Daniel. Even in exile, they were promoted! Look at how God blessed them through their mess. It would have been easy for the Hebrew boys to be discouraged because of their situation, but they served faithfully under Nebuchadnezzar. One day something dramatic happened. A huge image of gold was made in the middle of a plain in the province of Babylon. Nebuchadnezzar assembles everyone to worship the statue. He ordered, "As soon as you hear the sound of the horn, flute, zither, lyre, harp, pipe and all kinds of music, you must fall down and worship the image of gold that King Nebuchadnezzar has set up" (Daniel 3:5). Any opposition would be immediately thrown into a fiery furnace. Many saw the furnace and began to bow down and worship Nebuchadnezzar, but the three men refused to worship. Out of frustration, Nebuchadnezzar ordered the soldiers to make the fire seven times hotter, the highest it could go! The Hebrew boys still refuse to worship. The Hebrew boys were tied, and the king ordered for them to be thrown into the fire.

With a fire that hot, you would expect the boys to be instantly burned to death but look what happens next! Nebuchadnezzar confusingly investigates the fire. He said, "Look! I see four men walking around in the fire, unbound and unharmed, and the fourth looks like a son of the gods." (Daniel 3:25). Wait, four?!? We accounted for the three Hebrew boys, but who is this fourth person? It is Jesus! Jesus comes as an angel to protect the Hebrew boys! Jesus protected the men through the same mess that Nebuchadnezzar puts them in. Man may put you in a mess, but God will bring you out!

There are three lessons that we can pull from this moment to help you be encouraged even in your mess.

1. Jesus in Fire?

Talk about a mess! The same king who promoted the Hebrew boys in one season was about to have them killed. The good news is that the boys didn't put their faith in Nebuchadnezzar, their faith was in God! They told Nebuchadnezzar, "If we are thrown into the blazing furnace, the God we serve is able to deliver us from it, and he will deliver us from Your Majesty's hand" (Daniel 3:17). While others were focused on the fire, they focused on God! Whenever you are in a mess, who do you focus on? Man, or God? Shadrach, Meshach, and Abednego were so firm in their faith that they tell Nebuchadnezzar: "But even if he does not, we want you to know, Your Majesty, that we will not serve your gods or worship the image of gold you have set up" (Daniel 3:18). For them, no intimidation from the enemy would turn them away from God!

Now I have always thought about this: what if the Hebrew boys saw Jesus in the fire before they were thrown in? If they saw Jesus waiting for them, wouldn't they feel more comfortable being thrown in? Think back to Moses and the burning bush. To many, the moment would have seemed like there was a fire burning next to a bush in the wilderness. Which is typical, right? For Moses, it was the moment that he connected with God. Moses found God in the fire! Where others would have just seen fire, Moses saw God. I believe a similar instance happens with the three Hebrew boys. No matter how much faith they had, they probably were still afraid! Seeing that fire burning would have frightened me! What I believe happens is that the Hebrew boys looked deeper and found Jesus in the fire.

Understand, even though they found Jesus, they still had to go through the fire! In the world, you will still have to go through messes in life. Some messes that you can't even control. There will be times where it feels like the enemy has thrown you into the fire. The difference is that once you have found Jesus in the fire you can rest because He promises to protect you through the mess. Whatever troubled situation you may currently be facing, find God in the mess.

2. Walking in Fire

Nebuchadnezzar looks and sees the four people walking around in the fire. Clearly, Jesus came to protect the Hebrew boys in the fire, but why were they walking around in it? Why doesn't Jesus quickly guide them out of the fire? There was an important lesson that Jesus wanted to show them. When is the last time in the Bible that we see someone walking around something? Joshua and the Israelites in Jericho. God sends an angel to speak with Joshua (yes, another Christophany) about how to defeat Jericho. Joshua was instructed to walk around Jericho for seven days, and on the seventh day, the angel told him to walk around seven times. The walking had to seem redundant to Joshua after the fourth and fifth day. However, I believe God wanted them to understand the land they were about to possess!

God wanted Joshua and the Israelites to *"walk like they owned it."* The "it" was the Promised Land for Joshua. The "it" for you can be that interview, that business, or that class. When you are walking with God, you will begin to live your life more confidently because you have taken control of it. How does this relate to Jesus and the Hebrew boys walking around in the fire? Jesus wanted to show the boys that He owned death. Jesus foreshadows what happens on the cross! "O death, where is thy sting?" (Hosea 13:14). Death didn't affect Jesus because He had already defeated it! "For we know that since Christ was raised from the dead, he cannot die again; death no longer has mastery over him" (Romans 6:9). The Hebrew boys were confident in the fire because Jesus had nothing to fear in the fire!

Don't be afraid in your fire! If you have Jesus, you have nothing to fear! President Franklin Delano Roosevelt said, *"There is nothing to fear but fear itself."* Fear is simply an emotional reaction to a situation. You can control your fear! The good news is that when you are with Jesus in the fire you can be confident even amid your fears! If you have felt as if God has kept you in unfortunate circumstances, you should be encouraged! He is not keeping you there as punishment, but He is teaching you how to begin to take control of that situation. Once you take control of those situations, you will begin to live your life like you own it!

3. Refined by Fire

What irony it is that the person that puts the Hebrew boys into the fire is the one that orders them to come out! Nebuchadnezzar then approached the opening of the blazing furnace and shouted, "Shadrach, Meshach and Abednego, servants of the Most High God, come out! Come here!" (Daniel 3:26). Whenever the three boys came out of the fire, they didn't smell or look like what they had been through! You would expect third-degree burns everywhere on all three of them, but there was not a burn in sight! Nebuchadnezzar responded by not just celebrating them but also elevating them: "Therefore I decree that the people of any nation or language who say anything against the God of Shadrach, Meshach and Abednego be cut into pieces and their houses be turned into piles of rubble, for no other god can save in this way" (Daniel 3:29). Getting through the fire allowed the Hebrew boys to be elevated!

Whatever you believe God is using to punish you, He is using it to position you! Nebuchadnezzar elevated them because he was in awe of how they walked through the fire! Understand, people are watching HOW you get through your mess. Nebuchadnezzar was able to see God through the boys' walk because they never lost faith. You can't lose faith in this season. Whatever you may be facing, people are inspired by your endurance! The fire that you are going through is necessary to activate the purpose inside of you! God's not ignoring you. He is refining you!

Sometimes God puts you through the fire to remove things off of you. Remember when the Hebrew boys entered the fire, they were tied up, but when they came out there was nothing binding them! What is binding you in this season? What is the enemy trying to use to hold you hostage? A job, relationship, a church? The fire that happens could be God's way of removing those things from your life. Don't be depressed that you were let go from your job, God knew how much you hated it anyway! That person who left your life is God's way of positioning you to find your soulmate! The point is that God uses fire not to destroy, but to deploy! He is positioning you right now, through your mess, for greatness!

Thought: Mess is about perspective. Your situation may look messy because you are looking at it incorrectly, instead trust in God to help you through your current circumstance and watch change begin to happen.

9

The Purposeful Pursuit

Some people wake up daily in search of purpose. *"Why on earth am I here?"* Do you ever find yourself asking that question? You probably face this early in the morning when the alarm clock sounds, and you are headed to class or maybe your job. The search for meaning is what keeps us going in life. It is whenever you lose the desire to find meaning that things go awry. Most people search for purpose in the wrong places. The world today has prioritized social media over scripture to find purpose. We see how much money can be made from the number of followers we have, and it begins to drive us as a society. Instagram, Snapchat, and Twitter posts have served as the benchmark for success for many people worldwide.

Sadly, most of the posts that you see on social media are simply just a façade. You don't see what's actually "behind the post." Many people use these posts of "success" to cover up deeper issues. Our generation's attraction to social media has made other people's lives become our own gauge for success. Our minds are filled with *"I've got to make it just like him"* or *"I have got to save money, so I can get a house like that."* Two different problems occur when you have this mindset.

The first issue is that your focus is on worldly things, which are temporary. Once you've received your desires, your focus shifts to *"what's next?"* There is still a search for more in life, which means you will never truly be satisfied. The search for more worldly things takes your focus away from God. This is why Jesus said, "What good will it be for someone to gain the whole world, yet forfeit their soul? Or what can anyone give in exchange for their soul?" (Matthew 16.26). Numerous celebrities have obtained fame and fortune but still have trouble finding meaning in life. This is why suicide is so prevalent. People have a desire for more but are never truly satisfied. Remember, worldly things will only give temporary satisfaction.

Maybe that's not you. Well, let's look at the second issue with chasing after worldly things. What happens when God gives you exactly what you desire but in a different way? There are times we ask for things in life, but they don't come how we expect them to. We get angry because it is not exactly what we asked for. The issue is that we start to put our plans ahead of God's plans. When God takes you a different route, then you begin to question Him. Since things don't happen the way we expect, we mistakenly think God is not answering our prayers.

As you can tell, God's plans look a lot different than ours most of the time! Searching for purpose in the world is temporary and ultimately leads us to dissatisfaction. This is why the search has to start with Jesus. Look at Matthew 6:33. Jesus states, "But seek ye first the kingdom of God, and his righteousness, and all these things shall be added unto you." Jesus shows us that before searching for purpose you must first seek God. Before worrying about anything, God must be at the forefront of your life. Search for God first; then, He will begin to help you solve all of the other issues you may have.

The search for God is about understanding His righteousness. Searching for Him means faithfully walking with Him. Walking in the path of righteousness allows all the questions in your life to be answered. God teaches you through life experiences that you will find all of the other things you have been seeking. Remember, Jesus then says, "All these things shall be added unto you," which shows that all the emptiness in your life will be filled. Once you seek God, then that job you have been looking for or that person you've been dreaming about will all be manifested.

Let's stay in the Christmas spirit with this next chapter. We have looked at Christmas in the last chapter from Mary, the mother of Jesus. Let's look at the Christmas story, but from the wise men's perspective, the ones who searched for Jesus. To understand the story, we must start by talking about the wise men. The wise men were known as "Magi" or "kings." There have been debates about where the wise men originated from. Theologians say that they originated from Persia, and others say India. Whatever the case. What is crucial is that they come from a foreign territory. More than likely, the men followed the Armenian religious tradition. The wise men had different religious views and beliefs. However, despite their potential differences, they were all pursuing the same thing, Jesus.

The Wise Men

The wise men used the star of Bethlehem to find the "Coming Messiah." The wise men spent time studying to understand the fulfillment of the prophecy. Even when they saw nothing in previous seasons, they had to continue to believe that the prophecy would eventually come to pass. Conversely, we are a "see-it-to-believe it" generation. We see this with the constant debate over global warming. Since people can't see it with their eyes, they conclude that it doesn't exist.

Oftentimes, we miss opportunities simply because we lack preparation. Understanding requires preparation. The way that the wise men studied is similar to how we as Christians should study. God teaches us that we must meditate on His word day and night (Joshua 1:8, Psalm 1:2). Meditating on His Word allows us to be prepared. For the wise men, the preparation allowed them to see the arrival of Jesus, just as studying today prepares us for our reunion with Jesus.

The wise men also show us that every season of your life is crucial. We take certain seasons of our lives for granted. We say, *"Next year is my year!"* What about what God is trying to do for you this year? If you focus too much on what next season looks like, you will miss what God is trying to do for you this season. What if a farmer took one season for granted? How would that affect the harvest? The farmer would not be able to harvest all of their crops. The same thing applies to our lives. Every season is crucial because God teaches us something at every stage.

First, the wise men go to Jerusalem to ask King Herod about the birth of the Messiah. God leads the wise men to a dangerous place. Going to Jerusalem talking about the birth of the "King of the Jews" would be extremely risky because Herod is opposed to anyone who threatened the throne. Jerusalem is the same place where Jesus goes to be persecuted. So why did God lead the wise men to this place? God sends the wise men to Jerusalem to stir up the establishment. Think about it. Once the wise men even utter about the newborn king, Herod scrambles to find the answer to this "King of the Jews." Jesus caused havoc in Jerusalem before He even arrived!

There are times God puts us in certain positions where we are confused about His reasoning. Sometimes God places you in different environments to create a disturbance. The Bible says, "When King Herod heard this, he was disturbed, and all Jerusalem with him" (Matthew 2:3). On a molecular level, the way that matter changes states is if the molecules are disturbed. God creates disturbances to change the seasons of our life. The wise men were already aware of where to find this "King of the Jews." The trip to Jerusalem was just God letting the people know that the Savior was on the way! I know it feels like people are against you, and they don't even know you. Well, that's because your name has gone places you have yet to explore. God is creating a disturbance on your behalf! Herod calls the priests and the scribes to find the answer to where Jesus is born. He goes to people for the solution instead of God.

The disturbance that the wise men created, going through Jerusalem, only confirmed that they were headed in the right direction. Don't be shocked whenever God sends you through your enemies while you are searching for purpose. God uses the opposition to show that where you are headed is greater than where you have been.

Think about Nehemiah. The resistance that he faced only occurs whenever he is rebuilding the walls for the Lord. Take note of this!

Whenever you are rebuilding, you will always face opposition. Don't let opposition deter you; let it inspire you! God is letting you know that you are headed in the right direction. The enemy will always try to push hardest when you are close to your destination. Don't give up! The depression and anxiety you're facing could be confirmation that you are in the right place. God didn't say that the battles in your life wouldn't come. He just promises us that He will be our refuge during the battles. Your struggles only serve as the test in your testimony. Your pursuit of purpose is not easy. That's the reason it belongs to you and no one else. God designed it expressly for you, so He knows that you have the stamina and endurance to make it through.

Find the Light

So now the wise men are back on their quest to find the newborn king. The wise men use the light as their compass because the prophecy declares that the Savior would be born under the light. What's important to note is how they used the light to guide them. The light serves as a symbol of God's revelation. Not people's. Think about this, people didn't even realize who Jesus was when He was right in front of them. The fact that Mary had to give birth in a manger is further proof that people were unaware of Jesus' value. Many people won't understand the importance of where you're headed; therefore, it's crucial to let God give you direction. On their quest to find Jesus, they looked up and not out. We see with Herod what happens. He looked to people to find Jesus. People have their own opinion of "finding Jesus."

God reveals Himself in different ways throughout the Bible. The way God introduces Himself to Abraham is different than how He did for Moses. Nonetheless, what's similar in both men's stories is that they met God in the high place. In Biblical times the "high place" was where people would go to commune with God. David refers to the high place as "The Holy Mountain" or "Zion." So, in a sense, they "looked up" to find the presence of God. Now for us, this doesn't necessarily mean that everyone must go on a daily hike. However, I believe that the high place relates to the posture of our hearts. The highest place relates to how we see God. The humbling of our hearts and the exaltation of the Savior is how we can find Christ. Everyone in your life doesn't need to know where you're headed, just keep looking up, and watch God lead you!

The quest of the wise men was simply just a symbol of our daily walk with God. First, they had to be obedient to the light. Often, we have our own opinions of which way we should go in life. Whether this is with our career path or even our spiritual path, we get it in our heads that there is a specific path that we should walk. Look at the Israelites! It takes them forty years to be obedient to God's way for them. Don't extend your time in the wilderness! Understand that God will show you the path that He wants you to take once you seek Him. The choice is yours as to whether you will trust in the path that He has outlined.

The second thing that is powerful in the wise men's journey is trusting the process. I'd imagine that coming from the ancient near east it was hot! There weren't any fast-food restaurants to stop at when they were hungry. On top of that, we have already seen the disturbance they caused in Jerusalem. Theologians predict that they had to travel over 500 miles to find Jesus. There were probably moments that the wise men saw nothing but desert. There are similar moments in our lives when we find ourselves in a dry place. For the wise men, instead of focusing on the desert, they focused on the light.

Many times, we are in the gym and we have fitness goals outlined. After day three of your new High-Intensity Interval Training (HIIT) workout, there's some excellent news. Your body looks the exact same. Ha! You probably feel discouraged and are ready to quit. However, like the wise men, the result would make the journey worth it. In our quest to find our purpose, there will be times where things don't look promising. However, God just wants you to trust Him and trust the process.

The wise men finally arrive in Bethlehem. The Bible says, "When they saw the star, they rejoiced with great joy" (Matthew 2:10). There are a couple of questions that arise at this moment. Didn't the wise men notice the light when they were in the near east? Wasn't seeing the light the reason why they started traveling to Bethlehem? So why all of a sudden do they start feeling this way? Maybe they did see the light from afar. However, I believe that their joy came because they experienced in seeing the "light" up close. Sharing a personal encounter with Jesus will make you shout and rejoice. There was probably relief from the wise men that the One they were searching for was now found. There is gratitude knowing that the lost sheep are reunited with the true shepherd. This is the reason for worship. The wise men probably spent their entire lives searching for meaning and truth, and it was found in a manager with a baby wrapped in swaddling clothes.

Match the Energy

The wise men look into the manger, and they see Jesus. What's the first thing they do? They fell down and worshipped (Matthew 2:10).

Don't miss it!

They fell down first; then worshipped. So, the wise men humbled themselves before God, so that He could be exalted. Frequently, worship turns into a concert. We have become focused on the song or the performance, and we miss the reason behind our worship. Also, the wise men weren't too tired to worship. As stated in the previous section, they were said to have traveled over 500 miles. The wise men showed us that worship is not about us, but about the One who saved us, Jesus Christ.

Now, this is interesting!

We know that when they arrived at the manger, they were overcome with joy. Then, when they entered the stable, they worshipped. They found joy on the inside, and then they worshipped on the outside. So, the wise men's outward expression matched their inward expressions. My question to you is: are you happy that you have found Jesus in your life? If so, then your worship should reflect your gratitude and joy. There are times where we rejoice over unexpected money, a job promotion, overcoming sickness. However, what happens when things don't go well? Does your worship match? Are you still grateful and joyful? We have no idea what the wise men were dealing with. I believe that it is strategic because God is showing us that our internal and external worship of Him should match no matter what season we're in. The wise men understood the newborn king's value, and that was reason enough for them to worship.

To better understand, let's look back at David. We're going to analyze 1 Chronicles 13:8. At this point, David had gone to reclaim the Ark of the Covenant and bring it into Jerusalem. The Levites were responsible for carrying the ark because it held the presence of the Lord. The ark had to be dealt with properly. Until now, David avoided affiliating himself with the ark because Uzzah died touching it. Now, David was responsible for carrying the ark to the city of Zion. Look at David's response while carrying the ark. While David was bringing the ark, the Bible says, "Then David and all Israel played music before God with all their might singing, on harps, on stringed instruments, on tambourines, on cymbals, and with trumpets" (1 Chronicles 13:8). Like the wise men, David's and the Israelites' outside worship matched their inside joy.

We can learn from both instances that our worship is an essential part of purpose. Worship is not just about singing and dancing, but it is about the posture of your heart. The wise men and David both found something special; the wise men with the newborn king and David with the Ark of the Covenant.

As Christians, we have also found something special. Jesus died so that everyone could be saved from sin. God allowed all of us to receive Him through the resurrection of Jesus Christ. The Bible says, "Ye are of God, little children, and have overcome them: because greater is He that is in you, than He that is in the world" (1 John 4:4). We all have Jesus and that should be the reason for our worship!

Give Your Gift

After the wise men worshipped, they presented Jesus with gifts. The wise men gave the best of what they had to Jesus. They did not expect anything in return for their gifts. Why? The wise men realized that Jesus is the gift! In the Christmas season, our society has focused on giving and receiving the best gifts every year. Don't believe me? Turn on your TV and look at all the Christmas commercials - new toys, new appliances. new clothes. What's the common word? New. One of the enemy's tricks is to present us with shiny new objects to distract us from seeing Christmas' true meaning, God giving our world His Son. We get so caught up in worldly gifts that we miss the true gift of Christmas. Our focus must be on giving, not receiving.

Consider the different gifts that the wise men give Jesus. The wise men give Jesus gold, frankincense, and myrrh. Why is this important? All the gifts represent Jesus. The gold showed His royal status. The frankincense was used with sacrificial offerings to God, which Jesus represented as God in the flesh. Then they gave myrrh, which people used as embalming oil for the dead. So, the myrrh represented man, which Jesus embodied as well. God. King. Man.

The wise men's gifts all were indicative of the newborn king. So, in another sense, the wise men's gifts represented what they thought of Jesus. Ask yourself, how do the gifts I give represent the God I serve? With the gifts that God has given us, are we willing to give back to Him? The gifts don't just relate to money. What about our time? Or our energy? All the gifts that we have are because of God. When it's time to give it back to Him, our response is sometimes lackluster or "whatever I have left." The wise men didn't take the presence of the Lord for granted, and neither should we! That means that we should always look to give the best we have in everything. Just like David worshipped with all his might, we must look to give Jesus with all we have in every aspect of our lives.

A lot of times, we are expecting so much. Jesus, can you help me get this car? Jesus, PLEASE help me get out of this situation. Rightfully so, we turn to Jesus in times of need. However, the wise men did not ask Jesus for anything when they saw Him. Maybe it was because Jesus was a newborn. Or perhaps because they realized that they didn't need anything in return because Jesus was the gift. Jesus was God's ultimate gift to us because He loves us. If we have the wise men's posture, then we will be able to live life more peacefully. Everything that we get...money in our bank account...food to eat... car to drive...are all amenities, but God gave us all we need with Jesus. Our focus must shift to giving back to Jesus; only then, will He provide everything you have been waiting for, including your purpose!

Be Wise

One question I have always had when I read the story about the wise men: Why were they called "the wise men?" Why does the Bible refer to them as wise? Well, I believe that they were called wise men because they were pursuing Jesus. The wise men were seeking the right thing. The path to pursuing Jesus provides wisdom. Many times we chase after the wrong things in our lives. Maybe it is a job for some, and it might be that relationship you have been dreaming about for others. We are attempting to find truth and meaning in the search for these worldly things. However, we seem to come up short in the pursuit of purpose.

Activate Your Purpose

The wise men gave us the answer to how we activate our purpose in life. The search was so important to find Jesus. The search gave them wisdom, riches, and knowledge. All things that we hope and long for in life. Now I would imagine you are probably saying, *"Riches, where?"* The riches, in this case, are in the heart. Everything they have longed for was now answered through one name, Jesus. There has to be a pursuit of Jesus because that is where your purpose will be found. The phrase we use during Christmastime is *"Jesus is the reason for the season."* Yes, this is true, but let's look at it from a different angle. How about, *"Jesus is the reason for EVERY season?"* This mentality will allow you to pursue Jesus no matter what season you are currently in. There is power in the name of Jesus! The answer to your life's questions are found in Jesus. The choice is yours! If you are ready to activate the purpose that lies within you, then it's time to call on Jesus' name! Build your relationship with Jesus Christ, and He will activate the purpose God has planned for you!

There are many lessons that we can pull from the story of the wise men. The men give us a guide into how we must live while constantly pursuing truth and meaning. I have narrowed it down to three unique principles that I believe will help you go in the direction towards your purpose.

1. Just Do It

In a recent ad in conjunction with ex-NFL star Colin Kaepernick, Nike posted a quote that pointed towards identifying racial injustice in America. The quote reads, *"Believe in something. Even if it means sacrificing everything."* The world collectively stopped and admired the courage of both Kaepernick and Nike. Advertising boldness is nothing new for Nike. The company has a history of taking the initiative and pushing agendas with its advertisements. Nike has featured advertisements that encourage bridging the income gap for women in sports and even commercials spotlighting people with disabilities participating in sports. The theme of all their marketing is based on their slogan, "Just Do It." The slogan comes from an advertising campaign in 1988. The campaign targeted people of all ages, genders, and backgrounds to get active.

The idea centered around Nike's slogan is what I believe should for all of us. Think back to the story of the wise men. The wise men had to leave their respective nations. This means that in order for them to pursue Jesus, they had to give up their old way of life. Talk about a huge leap! What I believe the wise men understood was that there was no time to waste! When the prophecy was revealed, they had to go. Many times we are hesitant to follow God's instruction. Understand that delayed obedience is disobedience. God has already considered your past when He called you! People probably thought the wise men were crazy for leaving to go search for a baby. However, they knew they couldn't let obstacles deter them from their purpose. No matter where you might be in life, God wants you to come! Just do it!

2. Jesus Doesn't Discriminate

John 3:16 says, "For God so loved the world that he gave his one and only Son, that whoever believes in Him shall not perish but have eternal life." Read it again. The important part of this scripture is *"that whoever believes in Him."* This means that salvation is not limited to church people. Jesus died for everyone! He loves you AND me. Religious zealots will make you believe that you must have certain characteristics in order to have God's love. The truth is that God loved you before you were even born. The fact that God took time to create you should show you His love.

Delayed obedience is disobedience.

The interesting thing about the wise men is that we are unsure of their religion's affiliation. No matter the debate, it doesn't matter! Jesus came to save everyone. Even if they had different religious beliefs, how crazy is it that the prophecies still pointed to Jesus? So this means whether you are Muslim, atheist, or any other religion or non-religious, Jesus loves you. All God wants is for you to come to Him. The wise men fall down and worship by simply coming into the presence of God. The same thing can happen to you!

Look at the people God chooses. An adulterer. A murderer. A tax collector. All people who would more than likely be condemned and ostracized by society today. This shows that God can use you no matter your circumstances. Don't ever think you are unqualified. Remember God doesn't call the qualified, He qualifies the called!

Invite Jesus into your life. Your sexual orientation, race, past, and gender are no barriers for Jesus. The question is will you believe in Him. God's purpose for your life was created with all of your differences in mind. You are set apart for purpose! Culture will try to make you think that you must change in order to have a relationship with God. Nonsense! God wants you to have a relationship with Him right where you are, then He will make any necessary changes in your life.

3. Perception Guides Direction

This is one of my favorites. The principle you must always understand is, *"Perception guides direction."* Let me break it down. There's an apple at the grocery store. I envision using the apple to make delicious apple pie. You see the apple as simply just ... an apple. It's the same apple, but the apple is more valuable to me. Therefore, it is more likely that I will buy the apple and attempt to make the pie. There is nothing wrong with the person not buying the apple - you just didn't see the value in spending money on something they weren't going to use. Imagine this: What if Jesus is the apple? The way you see Jesus will determine how you pursue Him. People today have been led away from Jesus. This problem has occurred not because of Jesus, but because of how He is perceived.

Today many religions have been formed because of a difference in perspectives. Even within Christianity, there are a multitude of denominations because of unique perspectives about Christ. Think about it. The Pilgrims came to America because of their unique perspective. They envisioned America as a place where they could serve God in their own way. The most important thing to understand is that your purpose depends on your perspective. When you think about your purpose, what do you envision? Do you see it as something small? You will treat your purpose on the level of importance that you perceive it. The wise men didn't see their journey as a way to see a toddler. They were determined to see the King of the Jews. People saw a baby; the wise men saw as a king! They valued Jesus differently which is why they traveled over 500 miles to see Him.

Your perspective is dependent upon your mindset. Paulo Coelho stated it best, "If you think small, your world will be small. If you think big, your world will be big." The same applies to your purpose. The reason you are struggling to find your purpose isn't that it is lost, your mindset may be limited. God is a big God! We must think big as well! Once you see how big our God is then you will realize the size of your purpose because you are made in His image. Thinking big will allow you to get through adversity more easily because you serve a God who is bigger than the problem. Start telling your problems about our big God! I know you have probably heard that statement many times, but always keep this at the

---

Purpose depends on your perspective.

---

forefront of your mind. No one knows the totality of God because He is so profound! God reveals more about Himself to those who seek Him. The unknown parts of God make your spiritual journey worthwhile! Your constant pursuit of God will help you never stop growing. Your journey towards God will lead you towards your purpose. The impact on the world can either be big or small, it all depends on your perspective.

* * *

What's the Big Idea?

As you can tell, activating your purpose is a crucial part of finding your purpose. Your dreams and aspirations are clouded with the pains of life. It's hard to stay focused on the vision that God has given you when the world has presented so many obstacles on your path. Bills, toxic relationships, and doubting yourself are just a few of the roadblocks that you will encounter in your pursuit of purpose. How do you continue to search for your purpose when everything in the world distracts you? Two words...pirouette focus.

If you are weightlifting, you know the importance of focusing. Whenever you are using the squat rack in the weight room, the first thing that you should do is find a spot on the ceiling and keep your eyes on it. The minute that you take your eyes off of the spot problems happen. The amount of weight along with the position of your body has the potential to create major back and neck issues. In order to mitigate the risk, keep your eyes on the ceiling! Fixing your eyes on a point on the ceiling helps to keep your back straight! In life, you will feel like there's more weight that you are forced to carry physically and spiritually. Fix your eyes on God. Look up!

Spiritually, whenever you are burdened with the weight of the world, we must keep our eyes focused on "things above" instead of worldly things. If we keep our eyes focused on the world, we will encounter problems that can affect us in more ways than we can imagine. Instead, fix your eyes on Jesus! The enemy's trick is to use distractions to keep you from purpose, but keeping your focus on Jesus straightens your path. Jesus is the compass to point you towards your purpose! You trust your GPS to travel on your vacation, but do you trust Jesus to carry you to your destiny? Jesus is The Way! Look at what the author of Hebrews says:

"Fixing our eyes on Jesus, the pioneer and perfecter of faith. For the joy set before him he endured the cross, scorning its shame, and sat down at the right hand of the throne of God" (Hebrews 12:2).

We can fully understand how to activate our purpose by looking at the life of Jesus. As you continue your journey, I want to leave you with three principles to help you continue to walk faithfully on the path towards purpose.

1. Endurance requires Focus

Jogging sucks! I don't understand how people are able to run marathons because I can barely get to a mile. Running is so painful, but it is a great way to stay healthy and lose weight! One of the ways that I ease the struggles of running is focusing on a house or a sign far away, and the closer I get to the point that I set helps me to stay encouraged on my run. The point never changed, the only thing that changed was my perspective! What seemed far away suddenly became close once I chose to start moving. I would always tell myself before I ran, *"Just make it to the sign."* Once I passed the sign, I would choose another point and refocus. As we run the race towards Heaven, it is crucial that we set Jesus as our point and never take our eyes off of Him!

Due to the many circumstances in life, there are more times that we are running away from our problems more than we are running to Jesus. There must be a commitment to finding Jesus in the midst of the world! You can't always control what you see, but you can control what you fix your eyes on! Fix your eyes on Jesus. This doesn't mean what you actually see! If you look up right now you will see blue skies, but if you look with your heart you will see beyond with skies. Sight comes from your eyes, but vision comes from the heart! Whenever I run, looking with my eyes only shows what the sign says, but vision allowed me to see myself finishing the run. You are encouraged through your vision! Oftentimes, you can tell the people who lack vision because nothing ever excites them! When you have a vision, nothing can stop you until you achieve it!

As we run the race towards Heaven, it is crucial that we set Jesus as our focal point and never take our eyes off of Him! There is no coincidence, the writer compares our spiritual journey to a race, "And let us run with perseverance the race marked out for us" (Hebrews 12:1). Fixing your eyes on Jesus helps your endurance. Whenever you are challenged with the struggles of the world you can be encouraged because you are only getting closer to Jesus. Setting Jesus as your point will help you realize that He never changes, only we do.

2. Jesus, the Author

Harper Lee. J.K. Rowling. Jesus. What do all three of these people have in common? They are all authors. Yes, Jesus was an author. The writer of Hebrews describes Jesus as "the author and perfecter of our faith." Critics will probably say, *"what did Jesus even write?"* Jesus wrote the book of faith! Instead of writing any physical copies. Jesus wrote an entire book through His life. We can understand how to operate as Christians by looking at Jesus. From birth, Jesus faced opposition.

Jesus had to come to Earth and sell the idea of the coming kingdom. In order to promote the new Kingdom, Jesus started with absolutely nothing. No money, job, or people. He worked to build a team and His entire life was about helping others with their problems. Jesus' own people turn against Him. Jesus is tortured by Roman soldiers after being labeled as an insurrectionist. The sentence for His accusations is death. Even though Jesus could (and should) have given up, He still continued to live out the mission! How many obstacles would it take for you to give up on your mission? Whatever your answer maybe it doesn't compare to everything Jesus endured to accomplish His task. Jesus never even got to see the physical manifestation of the things that He sowed for thirty-three years. However, Jesus knew that everything would soon come to pass. His entire life was all centered on one thing...faith.

The faith of Jesus is something that every believer should note with their spiritual walks. Jesus specifically tells us, "In this world you will face trouble..." (John 16:33). The world is filled with adversity! There will be people blocking you from your purpose. I will put it this way: for every Moses, there will always be a Pharaoh. You must understand this, but don't let opposition stop you from purpose. The roadblocks in life are only meant to test our faith. I believe Jesus welcomed adversity because it strengthened His faith. Learn by observing Jesus' life. Then you will be able to stay focused on your purpose because no one can take away your faith. When you have faith like Jesus, you will spend less time worrying about your storms and more time sleeping through them.

3. Find the Joy

When you have faith like Jesus, you will spend less time worrying about your storms and more time sleeping through them.

Do you have joy? Are you that grumpy friend that no one ever wants to be around? There are a lot of people that you see today who don't have joy. Happiness and joy are two different things. Happiness is short-term and is typically based on a circumstance. You can hear it in people's statements: *"I'm happy because I just got my refund check."* Conversely, joy is not based on circumstance. You have joy in spite of your circumstance: "I just failed that test, but the enemy won't take my joy." See the difference? Joy is a fruit of the Spirit (Galatians 5:22) - meaning that you can have joy from wherever you are!

The most joyful book in the Bible is Philippians. Interestingly, Paul pens the letters that make up this book in prison. Could you imagine being chained and then saying, "I shall abide and continue with you all for your furtherance and joy in faith" (Philippians 1:25)? Paul didn't let his situation steal his joy. There are many things in your life right now that are trying to steal your joy. Gossip, doubt, and comparing yourself to others are all mines that are waiting to explode and steal your joy. You have to make a conscious effort to avoid these traps of the enemy! You must *choose joy*!

Jesus knew there was more to the cross than just wood and nails. While everyone saw the cross as the end, He saw it as the beginning! This was His opportunity to reconvene with the Father! Jesus had every right to be negative because of His circumstance. He was smitten, stricken, and afflicted for telling the truth for God's sake! Instead of dwelling on the pain and agony, He focused on the *"joy set before Him."* Jesus found joy in His situation. There is joy in everything in life, you just have to find it! How you see the situations in your life will determine your emotional response. Think about all the good things that came from Jesus' death: He was able to go and *"sit at the right hand of the Father,"* believers were filled with His Spirit, and the church spread all over the earth. I believe that finding the joy in His situation helped Jesus get through all of His sufferings. As believers, we too will also face suffering throughout our life. The good news is that when you understand the purpose behind your suffering, you can have joy in the midst of suffering.

10

Unlocking Starts with U

You have seen various examples of how others were able to activate their purpose. Now, I want to give you my own account. For many years of my life, I struggled with the universal question discussed in this book, *"What am I on earth for?"* At this time, instead of asking these questions to God, I attempted to answer them myself. I tried to find meaning in a multitude of ways.

Coming into college, I was very interested in entrepreneurship. I loved the way that one could identify a problem, solve it, and turn it into a billion-dollar company. Solving the problems in this world has always been my focus. It was always a struggle sitting in class every day listening to a lecture. I doodled on my iPad business ideas and started to plan out my life after undergrad. I successfully started my company, Ventful, and it was a mobile app to find local events. From the start, everything seemed to work out. I found the team, successfully built the app, and even got it on the App Store. Everyone celebrated our success with the app. People started to highlight us as a potentially successful startup company.

At the same time that I started the company, I also joined a fraternity. After joining the fraternity, it immediately changed my social life. Most of my weekends were spent with fraternity events and obligations. Another feature associated with fraternities is the social life...like parties. Seeing other people having fun made me believe that this would help me to find myself.

What resulted was me being stuck mentally, physically, and spiritually. I struggled to find myself even more. The emptiness inside of me seemed to be growing. Nothing that I was doing was satisfying. My company faced issues finding money and scaling. On top of all of those issues, my grades suffered. I chose to put on a mask with people to hide how I was truly feeling. There came a point where I contemplated suicide because I felt my life had no meaning. I began to seclude myself from everyone, to include my parents. Many attempts were made to help my mood to change, but inside these attempts were all pointless.

At my lowest point, I gave everything to God, and it changed my life forever. I began to watch sermons and read my Bible. Weeks later, I began to feel much better. As I studied the Bible and spent more time in church, I realized that ministry was my calling. I love anytime that I can analyze and preach the Gospel. I started a ministry with my friends called, "The 412." The ministry was based on 1 Timothy 4:12, "Don't let anyone look down on you because you are young, but set an example for the believers in speech, in conduct, in love, in faith and in purity." Our goal was to bring authenticity back to Christianity. The same place where I struggled to find myself, a year later, is where I began ministry. Our ministry showed me that there were more people who faced the same issues as me. The world is filled with people who don't know their purpose, nor are they seeking their purpose which amounts to wasted days.

God gave me the concept of "activate your purpose" in a moment that I needed to be spiritually revitalized. He used the circumstances in my life to show me the problems that most of the world is dealing with. I realized that people's souls are lost because they are chasing their dreams without God. For me, it was my startup company, Ventful. It may be something completely different for you. When God is not the focus, issues arise. This is the problem we see with the Tower of Babel. God didn't tell them to build it, and as a result, it didn't work out. The same will happen for anyone who focuses on building something without God. Everything in your life will feel scattered. Despite the confusion in my life, God gave me direction. Everything that I went through motivated me to discover and activate my purpose in life. Change starts with you. The purpose for my life was not revealed until I chose to put my faith in God. Understand this! Unlocking your potential starts with you! God has given you the power to change your situation. In order for change to occur, you must first trust in Him! After many conversations, I have concluded that it's not that people don't know what they want to do with their life, but more so how they are supposed to do it. We have all been there! We forget that between God telling Noah to build the ark and having a finished product, there were steps in between! Purpose is not hard to understand. Your interests and abilities will point you to what you are called to do. It takes obedience and intuition for it to become fruitful. The purpose of this book is for you to understand both sides. My hope is that you not only find your purpose, but that you do what is necessary to bring it to life!

As you probably have realized since you have gotten to this part of the book, there are many aspects of activating purpose. Don't feel overwhelmed. Some of the topics may not necessarily apply to you right now. Maybe you feel like you need to improve in one area more than another. Lean into the chapter that suits you the most right now. You might be in the fight of your life, struggling to understand your purpose. Lean into, *The Purpose Battlefield*. If that is

---

Change starts with you.

---

not you then what about if you're trying to figure out why you keep going through the same cycles year after year. Skip back to *Paralyzed Purpose*. The point is, at some point in your life, you will experience each chapter. Take some time to reflect on each season to figure out what chapter is the most applicable in that season. Open this book again if you need to and continue to see how it relates to each season of your life. Don't be fooled! Activating your purpose is not just a one-time thing! It occurs many times in your life. There are a lot of times where God may be calling you to something different.

Understanding how to navigate each topic is crucial for your overall development as a leader. Success starts with activation. Even if you experience these topics at different points in your life, whenever you face any of the chapters discussed you will be aware that you are in an activation season. God is simply waiting for you to activate the purpose that He has for you in that season.

Despite everything discussed in the book, you must understand that you are the key to unlock your purpose. This book only serves as a guide to give you direction to your purpose. Taking steps to get there depends on you. What steps will you take to activate your purpose? Your purpose is waiting for you. It's up to you to find it. Don't be discouraged. If Gideon, Moses, and many other leaders were able to find their purpose, so can you!

* * *

The tools that we have discussed can be summed up into three different steps. I want to leave you with these points that are essential in your life's journey. Follow these steps and activate your purpose.

Success starts with activation.

1. Don't Give Up

Finding your purpose is easy, but actually understanding what to do with your purpose is the hard part. It is crucial that despite adversity that you don't give up on activating purpose. Let's go to the Old Testament in order to examine a leader who doesn't give up on his purpose. After Moses' death, Joshua takes the helm as the leader of the Israelites. His task now is to guide the Israelites into the Promised Land. Whenever he arrives, Joshua encounters a great wall. It had to be discouraging to be at the cusp of God's promise only to be met by another obstacle. Joshua attempts to find a way to get past the wall. He even sends spies and consults with them about the best strategy. God sends an angel to give Joshua instructions about conquering Jericho. You probably already know the story of Joshua and the Battle of Jericho but there are some key points in the story that I want you to understand. First, even though Joshua is near the promise it was not immediately given to Him. There is still work that must be done! Activation must occur. It wasn't just about the physical location for Joshua and the Israelites. God wanted their heart, soul, and mind all to be aligned. How does God accomplish this? He instructs them to walk. God says, "March around the city once with all the armed men. Do this for six days" (Joshua 6:3). Think about your dream job. What if God tells you to do this same thing around the building before you even apply? More likely than not you would question God. *"Why would God make me do that over again and again?"* God wanted the Israelites to believe that Jericho was theirs before He gave it to them.

Just like we discussed in *Paralyzed Purpose*, God wants to change you inside and out. The important thing to understand, no matter how long it took, Joshua never gives up. Even when God tells Joshua to walk around the same building seven times on the seventh day. Talk about tired! Joshua's relentlessness is key to him activating his purpose. Being relentless is the key to your life as well. The enemy wants you to give up and lose your drive. Joshua probably walked and thought, *"this can't be worth it"* or *"it is way too hot for this."* Not only did he push through physically, but he also endured mentally. Don't let your thoughts cause you to give up on your purpose! God has a special plan for you, but to get there you must endure and trust in God's process.

2. Don't Give In

We discussed in the previous section about not giving up on your purpose. Unfortunately, there is something that is equally as dangerous...giving in. As mentioned in *Paralyzed Purpose*, one of the enemy's main tricks is lying. The enemy fabricates every story to make you look at your situation differently. The key is not to give in to the enemy's lies. To identify a lie, you must know the truth. To understand the truth, you must understand the source—this process is called discernment, which comes from the Holy Spirit. Discernment divides reality from lies. Like the theme throughout the book, this process must be activated! It starts with you. Invite the Holy Spirit in so that He can begin to lead you on the path of truth.

Now the enemy is not ignorant. Most of the time the enemy won't just tell a flat-out lie. Sometimes "giving in" isn't just about feeling fooled by a lie but can also come from distractions presented by the enemy. One of the best ways that I have heard how to combat distractions is with the "beeline principle." Dr. Calvin Mackie, uses the "beeline principle" to educate people on eliminating distractions. He says that you must form a beeline to where you intend to go whenever you are in the mall to avoid the distractions of kiosks and food courts.

When you think about going to the mall, you are usually going for one thing. Maybe it's a computer from Best Buy or a suit from Belk. Get in and get out. What ends up happening is that hours go by, and you are still walking around in the mall. The reason? Distractions. There are endless kiosks and mannequins in the window that are intended to get our attention. Even the smell of pretzels and cookies often causes us to be distracted. Often, we leave the mall, not even getting the thing that we came in for. In life, we face many distractions. There are "kiosks" that stop us along the way that distracts us from our purpose. Maybe your purpose is a new job. Another job offer is presented to you and the base salary forces you to rethink everything. It looks and feels good, but is it truly good for you?

Don't be distracted by the interruptions but focus on the end goal. Mackie uses the mall as an analogy but relates it to our life. We cannot stop at every distraction in our lives because it will waste time from getting to our purpose. To tackle how not to give in we will look at someone who does the exact opposite. In the garden, Eve was approached by a serpent. The serpent presents her with lies to convince her to eat the forbidden fruit. How does he do this? The serpent asks her a question. He says, "Did God say, 'You must not eat from any tree in the garden'?" (Genesis 3:1). The first key in spotting a lie is the enemy tries to make you question yourself. Eve replies based on what she heard from Adam. However, the enemy lies to her and tells her that eating the fruit would make her "like God" (Genesis 3:5). After she eats the fruit, she influences her husband to eat the fruit as well. As a result, they are both banished from the garden for disobeying God.

What can we learn from this story? The enemy's ultimate goal is to turn you away from God. You must be conscious that the closer you get to God, the more you will face the enemy's attacks. Why? You have influence. Look at how much influence Eve had by convincing her husband (who is supposed to lead) to eat the fruit! The reason that you are facing distractions in this season is that you have influence. The enemy's strategy is to trick you so that you can influence others to be fooled as well. Also, seeing a snake in a garden is typical. The enemy is strategic with deception. The enemy selects a serpent because it would seem familiar to Eve whenever it is spotted. Be careful!

You need to identify the "serpents" in your life. There are some things that you may think belong, but they really don't, and the enemy attempts to distract you from your purpose. The serpent for your life might be money. Are you letting your bank account lie to you about what you need? Don't let what seems natural cause you to do something unnatural.

Wherever you are in your life, you can still make a beeline. Take some time and think about what God has called you to do. Write it out. Once you have figured it out, then decide about how you plan to achieve it. Then, form the beeline. Don't stray away from what you wrote unless God leads you elsewhere. The discipline will allow you to eliminate wasted time because you have passed up all of the distractions around you. Stay focused, and don't give in. Your purpose depends on your focus!

3. Don't Settle

Out of all the "Don'ts" that we have discussed, this is the one that I want you to understand the most. Let me give you some insight into another strategy of the enemy. Whenever the enemy can't take you out, he will try to make you settle. The enemy knows how impactful your purpose is to the world. So, in order to combat this, he strategically places obstacles in front of you to lure you away from your purpose. The lure can be a multitude of things - could be with your spouse or even with your job. Whenever you settle in life, it causes you to become stuck. This is why the phrase "midlife crisis" is popular. People go their entire lives chasing money and status and realize they went opposite of their purpose. In your life, the enemy may be presenting you with lures right now. Don't settle! Is there a specific area in your life where you know you could do better? If the answer is yes, then you have probably settled.

Let me break it down further. There is a moment in the life of a young prophet named Daniel where the enemy intended for him to settle. Daniel and his friends served in King Nebuchadnezzar's palace. Before they were served, the king ordered Ashpenaz, chief of his court officials, to train Daniel and his friends for three years. Part of the training included them eating a daily amount of food and wine from the king's table. Sounds great, right? The best food and drink in the nation right in front of you in exchange for you serving the king. Look at Daniel's response! Daniel chooses not to eat the king's food and wine. He says, "Please test your servants for ten days: Give us nothing but vegetables to eat and water to drink" (Daniel 1:12). If you were Daniel's friend, would you be mad at Daniel? Cornbread, pork chops, and red velvet cake all gone because of Daniel. Ha! The important thing is that Daniel didn't want to settle for the king's food.

We discussed in *Designated Deliverer*, the dangers of intoxication when chasing purpose. What Daniel realizes is that eating the king's food would be intoxicating. It has nothing to do with the food, but all about the mindset. Daniel wasn't concerned about the food itself, but the source from which it came. The danger was that they would confuse their nourishment from Nebuchadnezzar instead of God. A lot of times we fall into the same trap in our lives. We look towards Uncle Sam or the President for help financially. We thank the Pastor for healing, and constantly check models on Instagram to find out ways to improve your appearance. All of these can become the "Nebuchadnezzar" of your life. The result is that it draws your focus to worldly things and turns your attention away from God. When you feel like you're heading in that direction, tell yourself, *"Don't settle!"*

Daniel turning down the king's food actually improves his appearance. Look at what The Bible says, "At the end of the ten days they looked healthier and better nourished than any of the young men who ate the royal food" (Daniel 1:15). So Daniel's decision not to settle led to him looking, and probably even feeling, better than his counterparts. In addition to his appearance, not settling also helped Daniel to fight his battles. See, Daniel and his friends not defiling themselves with the king's food showed how much he was dependent on God. We know the story about the three Hebrew boys. I believe that the Hebrew boys made it through the fiery furnace (Daniel 3:16), and Daniel made it out of the lion's den (Daniel 6) because they didn't settle earlier in their lives.

On your pursuit toward purpose, remember don't ever settle for less than God's best for your life. It's so easy to settle! Whatever your Nebuchadnezzar is trying to feed you, don't consume it. Ask God for discernment and follow His plan. Whenever you feel discouraged, remember what Jesus says in John 13:7: "You don't understand now what I am doing, but someday you will." Even though the things in front of you may seem enticing, what God has in store for you is much more rewarding. Don't settle!

11

Fulfilled Purpose

September 7th, 2020 was one of the most challenging days of my life. It was the day that my grandfather passed away. I was driving back to my apartment, and something inside of me said, "*Check on Grandma.*" I called and spoke with her, but something just didn't feel right after our conversation. As I approached my apartment, God spoke to me and said, "*It is finished.*" I instantly began to think about Jesus on the cross whenever He says these three words. I was confused about how the statement applied to my life. Hours later, my mother came to see me and told me the news. Once she told me, I thought about what God said to me and knew it was about my grandfather. First, I was devastated, but that soon changed because I realized that it was not a moment of sadness, but of celebration.

Whenever Jesus says, "It is finished" (John 19:28-30), He is on the verge of dying on the cross. The question becomes, "*What is the 'it' that Jesus is referring to?*" "It" represented His purpose! Jesus came to Earth to save the lost. He came to save, sanctify, and cleanse all of us. In order to complete this task, He had to sacrifice Himself. When Jesus utters these three last words, there was no point in trying to hold onto His life any longer because what He had sought to do was accomplished.

Thinking about this moment with Jesus, I thought about my grandfather. My grandfather had been sick for over a year. Despite his sickness, the one thing that he never worried about was death. In fact, in his last moments, he said, *"You know we aren't staying here forever."* My grandfather was at peace with his situation. He taught me that whenever you have lived a good life, you can handle death. Contrary to popular belief, living a good life is not about money or status, but about purpose! Even before my grandfather was sick, he continued to work well past the age of retirement. While everyone was begging him to retire, he continued to go to work daily. In addition to his work life, he faithfully served his church. There would be many times I would ride with my grandfather to church. I would watch him teach Sunday School, and occasionally he would take me downstairs to see how the deacons talk about church business. My grandfather was happy doing this every week because he was living out his purpose! Through my grandfather, I witnessed purpose truly activated!

The one thing my grandfather always believed in was servant leadership. Everyone knew that my grandfather was a leader. In the military, the classroom, and even in the church, he was the leader. However, the way that he led was in the background. Like Jesus, my grandfather was adamant about his service to his family and the community. He never wanted any credit for the things he did, but was also the first to help anyone in need!

After my grandfather's funeral, I was doing Bible study to stay encouraged in the midst of adversity. There was one verse that stood out to me. Psalm 138:8 says:

"The Lord will fulfill his purpose for me; your steadfast love, O Lord, endures forever. Do not forsake the work of your hands."

As I reread the verse, the one part that stood out to me was, *"The Lord will fulfill his purpose for me."* I thought to myself, *"fulfilled purpose."* Then, suddenly, God revealed to me that activation is the step before fulfillment. Jesus activated His purpose for thirty-three years on this Earth, and it was fulfilled with these last few words on the cross.

Activating your purpose is not the end, it's just the beginning! Activation is the first step toward fulfillment. Let me break it down further. As an undergraduate student at Clemson University, I majored in Industrial Engineering. One of my favorite classes was Transportation and Logistics. In the course, we mapped out the processes from raw materials to finished goods. To begin the process, we first had to identify the suppliers and manufacturers. Next, we mapped the process down the assembly line. Once the product was manufactured, distributors will take it to what is known as a fulfillment center. The fulfillment center is the place where the inventory is stored. From there, distribution is planned to fulfill customer's orders in a timely fashion.

I know you are probably reading this thinking, *"what does this have to do with my purpose?"* In life, there are times where we go into seasons too quickly. We go from activation to distribution. Even though you feel as if you have activated the purpose that God has for you, God is still positioning you to distribute your gifts to the world. Fulfillment is about priority. Whenever distributors come to fulfillment centers they collect inventory based on time, cost, and other factors, they understand that timing is just as important as quality. In your life, there are times where we try to skip over the fulfillment stage and go straight to distribution. You attempt to take the "leap of faith" when God is still telling you to wait. You quit your job to start that business, but God still wanted to teach you important lessons from your old job. Whenever you skip the fulfillment stage in life, you become unorganized and end up doing the right thing at the wrong time.

I'll give you an example. With the first pick of the 2020 NFL Draft, the Cincinnati Bengals drafted Joe Burrow. Two years before, no one in the world knew who he was. As a backup at Ohio State University, Burrow rarely saw any playing time. Burrow was a talented quarterback but was forced to sit behind other talented quarterbacks ahead of him. Due to his lack of playing time, Burrow transferred to Louisiana State University.

The minute that he arrived at LSU, everyone knew that he was a leader. Head coach Ed Orgeron even recalled that Burrow led a players-only volunteer practice to prepare for the next season. Joe was a great player and a natural leader! His hard work paid off by winning a national championship his senior season. Also, he signed a four-year deal with the Bengals for $36.2 million! Burrow bet on himself, and it paid off. At the beginning of his college career, it looked like Burrow was living his purpose. However, leadership doesn't happen overnight. Therefore, Burrow had to possess the same leadership displayed at LSU when he was at Ohio State. We can assume, based on his leadership and ability, that he was in the right place. However, God had different plans. God made him wait to develop not only as a player but also as a leader. Whenever he went to LSU, Joe already knew how to deal with adversity because he faced it throughout his collegiate career. God opened up the opportunities not only with LSU but also in the NFL draft. What most college quarterbacks try to do in four years of college, Joe was able to accomplish in two years!

You must trust God with the timing of your life. There will be many times where you feel slighted and overlooked, but God has you there for a reason. David, who wrote many psalms, faced this issue his entire life! Don't feel like you are behind in life, while watching [as] other people [are] get picked before you. God's timing is perfect! Trusting in Him will allow you to be in the right place at the right time! While others are seeing incremental growth, God is positioning you for exponential growth.

Jesus could have easily gotten down from the cross, defeated the Romans, and continued to spread the Gospel. The only problem is that it wasn't His purpose. Jesus trained the 12 Disciples for this moment. He wanted to pass the responsibility to others so that the church would spread throughout the entire world. Can you imagine how long it would have taken Jesus to get to every part of the world? Decades! The timing of Jesus' ministry was strategic. Think about it. God sent Jesus to Earth during the peak of the Roman dynasty. Rome was the capital of the world! The spread of the Roman empire was not just about power but also influence. Much of the philosophy and inventions created by the Romans are still used today. The Roman Empire was a microcosm of the Kingdom of God. During the 400 years between the Old and New Testaments, God could have sent Jesus to save the world from sin. God placed Him in the world at that specific time because it was the best time to introduce and spread the Gospel to the world.

Through Jesus' death, we see the spread of Christianity begin to infiltrate Roman culture. Look at Roman leader Cornelius being converted to Christianity (Acts 10)! God positions Jesus to save the world in only three years! Jesus waited on God's timing and was able to be more efficient with ministry. Remember that God wants you to live an abundant life. An abundant life is not only about being blessed but also sustaining the blessing. Don't just walk into seasons knowing your purpose; wait on the Lord so that He may fulfill your purpose!

What does it mean to be filled with purpose? Have you ever been to a restaurant and have eaten something good, but it wasn't quite filling? On many occasions, I have been there with those expensive restaurants, where you get fancy plates and small portions of food. It makes me sick! In certain seasons of our life, we can be doing things that look good externally but lack substance internally. God wants you to be satisfied internally and externally. You must lean into what God wants you to do! It may not seem like the best option, but God knows that it is the very thing, place, or person that will satiate your body, mind, and soul.

* * *

To help you stay encouraged as God fulfills His purpose for you, I want to leave you three lasting principles. These are three things I learned from my grandfather. Two I learned while he was still living, and one I knew the moment he left. These three principles will give you tangible steps toward fulfillment. Remember that activation is only the beginning of fulfillment!

1. Just Drive

My grandfather always used to take me on trips whenever I came to visit him. Typically, we would spend a weekend going to Myrtle Beach, South Carolina, about a 45-minute drive. There was one trip that stood out. We were coming back home from the beach, and I looked out of the window watching cars pass. I was furious because I had the rest of my day planned out, but my grandfather seemed to be driving so slowly! He played his jazz music and drove casually. After watching the eighth and ninth car pass, I tapped my grandfather on the shoulder and asked him why he was going so slowly. He turned around, laughing, and said, "*I am just driving.*" I disapproved of his answer, and I looked at the speed-o-meter, and shockingly he was going the speed limit! Everyone else was driving much faster! Afterward, he shared something with me so profound. I remember to this day, he told me, "*In life, it's not about how fast you get to your destination, just make sure you get there!*" At the time, it went in one ear and out the other. However, this continues to encourage me throughout my life!

You must realize that your purpose in life is never fully realized until the end. Essentially, you don't realize the impact that you have had until you look back throughout your life. It is so easy to get caught up in milestones that you don't value the process of life. Usually, it takes people to have some scary moments to appreciate the beauty of life. Don't let this be you! Whenever my grandfather drove, he knew every landmark and every building because he took everything in on the road trip. This even translated to the rest of his life. He had many connections because he valued the people he met along the way. People who tell you that "*it is lonely at the top*" are usually the very ones who were so caught up in the journey that they missed the people along the way. The reality is that the top should be crowded with all of the people you lifted along the way.

During my senior year of high school, I attended a basketball camp at Emory University. I had a great camp! I led my team in scoring and rebounding every game that we played. All the assistant coaches came up to me and asked where I was from and if any other schools were scouting me. I was excited because I knew that I would be leaving the camp with a scholarship in my hand. After the last game, the head coach came to meet me. As he shook my hand, I was waiting for him to say the words, "*we would like to offer you a scholarship.*" However, the coach said, "*enjoy the journey.*" I was confused, and I began to wait to see if he had anything else he had to say. Instead, he shook my hand and spoke to my parents, and left. After seeing my disappointment, my dad said it was important for me to understand the coach's words. My dad said, "*enjoying the journey is not just about basketball, but also about life.*" Enjoy the journey of life! Think about a roller coaster. When you ride a roller coaster, you don't think about the ride's ups and downs. If you focus on going up and down on the ride, you will miss the experience. The ups and downs together make roller coasters an enjoyable experience! On the roller coaster of life, there will be plenty of ups and downs. If you focus too much on the details, you miss the picture! Don't dwell too much on your mistakes and failures! God is using everything in life to fulfill your purpose. All you must do is just drive! Each day continue to live and trust the roads that God has already prepared for you!

2. Stay Positive

Every time I would visit my grandfather, he was a man of few words. His stoic demeanor meant that whenever he did speak, it was usually impactful. Once everyone got ready to leave, he would always remind everyone, "*stay positive.*" My grandfather would say this because he knew once we left his house, we would reenter the world, full of stress and anxiety. Many times in my life I found myself leaning on my grandfather's words for encouragement. What I now realize is that positivity is about perspective! Every situation in your life can be positive or negative depending on how you look. If this is true, then why not focus on the positive! Too many times in life, we focus on the negative. The enemy wants us to concentrate on the bad things in life because it will take our focus away from all of the good things. Whenever negativity surrounds you, it affects your faith. You will begin to focus on your obstacles more than God!

I witnessed this firsthand at the NCAA basketball tournament in Charlotte, NC. The number one seed Virginia Cavaliers played the

Enjoy the journey of life!

sixteenth-seed University of Maryland Baltimore County (UMBC) Retrievers. If you have never heard of UMBC, do not feel bad because that night no one had heard of them before either! As the game started, UMBC got out to an early lead, and the spectators in the arena were so excited to see the chaos that was brewing. As we watched, we knew UMBC had the opportunity to make history because this was the first time that a #16 seed would beat a #1 seed. Towards the end of the game, Virginia fans began to leave the arena because the game started to turn against their favor. I sat beside an avid Virginia fan, and he wasn't too pleased about the game's outcome. One thing that stuck with me was when he said, *"UMBC played to win, but we [Virginia] played not to lose."*

Are you currently living to win or living not to lose? There is a difference. Playing not to lose means that you focus on the negatives and eliminate as many as possible. Conversely, playing to win means that you focus on the positives of life and lean into them to win. Virginia didn't want history to be made against them, so they were conservative with their game plan. UMBC had nothing to lose; therefore, the players gave everything they had to win. Focusing on the positives helps you to approach life with more optimism. You will confidently pursue more opportunities and take advantage of moments in your life. Yes, it is crucial to be conservative sometimes, but playing to win is vital. Once you focus on playing to win, you will confidently pursue more opportunities and take advantage of moments in life.

Think about Jesus when He feeds 5000. The circumstances seemed unfavorable. More than five thousand people with only two fish and five loaves of bread looked almost impossible. However, look at what Jesus does whenever He gets the food: "Taking the five loaves and the two fish and looking up to heaven, He gave thanks and broke the loaves" (Matthew 14:19). Jesus thanks God for what He currently had instead of worrying about the circumstance. He focuses on the positive instead of the negative. God responds because of His outlook on the situation. In your life, what things are you looking at the wrong way? Respond to what seems impossible with positivity! God will not only solve your problems but will exceed your expectations. Every time you are faced with negativity in your life, remember to stay positive!

3. Pass the Baton

If you have ever watched track and field, then you have probably seen a relay race. The most important part of the relay race is the exchange. In high school, I would watch the runners prepare before the race. What shocked me, seeing them prepare, was there was no running! The players would speed walk around the track focusing on getting the exchange right. Other teams would be focused on the start and getting out of the block correctly. Whenever the race began, the difference was clear. Many of the groups dropped the baton and began to argue with each other. Later, I learned that if you dropped the baton, you were automatically disqualified from the race. Meanwhile, the team that prepared with the exchange won the race by a considerable margin. The exchange is not just crucial in track, but also life!

Leadership is not just about the legacy you live, but also the legacy you leave. Those after you will understand the impact of your life. Everyone should have something to pass on after they leave the Earth. If you haven't built something that outlasts you, then you must keep building! There comes a "moment of truth" in your life, where it is time to pass the baton. Messing up the exchange can potentially set your legacy back. There are many times where people have passed the baton to the wrong people. The wrong people can mishandle your baton, which causes your legacy to be affected. God will assist with the process of giving and receiving the "baton" of life. You must trust God with this process!

Passing the baton will take your legacy to the next level. The "next level" is essential to any person, business, or organization. To get to the next level in life, you must be willing to make painful decisions. If you get too comfortable, your legacy may never get to the next level because you are complacent on your level. I genuinely believe this is why a transition had to happen in the wilderness between Moses and Joshua. Moses didn't help any with striking the rock (Exodus 17:6). However, I believe that transition was necessary because Joshua could take the Israelites to the next level. The two men had a difference in mindset. Joshua's focus was getting to the Promised Land, while Moses focused on freeing the Israelites from slavery. Even though ultimately both were working toward the same goal, Moses' leadership was limited.

On the other hand, Joshua had been to the Promised Land; therefore, his experience elevated his mindset. He not only could sell the Promised Land to the Israelites through speech like Moses, but he experienced it! Moses recognizes this and understands that transition was necessary. The important thing to understand is that Moses didn't try to hold on to his position as a leader any more or less than he needed to. He passed the baton when God told him to, and it helped Joshua to accelerate into the Promised Land.

How do you pass the baton? Look at Jesus. Even though the baton usually relates to a business or organization, it is found through people. Whenever Jesus talks about the church He would leave, it was never about any physical building. Jesus built it through the leaders that he developed. One of the people that Jesus successfully passes the baton to is the early church leader, Peter. Jesus started by

---

Leadership is not just about the legacy you live, but also the legacy you leave.

---

preparing Peter to join Him in ministry. Even though Jesus knew that Peter would be His successor, He was secure enough to lead Peter. As a leader, you must not be insecure! You should always be willing to surround yourself with people who are also leaders. Surrounding yourself with leaders will challenge you to be a better leader! Don't keep a bunch of "yes" men in your corner because it will limit you as a leader along with your purpose.

Once Jesus identifies Peter, he then develops him. How does Jesus develop Peter? He challenges Peter. There are multiple instances where Peter is challenged: casting the net, walking on water, confessing his faith. Jesus knew that Peter would be the one to accept all of these challenges, and it helped Peter to develop as a leader. Once you have identified the people, you must challenge them through life's experiences. My grandfather would do this in multiple ways. One of the ways he would do this is to ask me questions randomly about stocks and investing. At first, I was unclear about the terminology, along with the questions that he asked. The confusion motivated me to read more about investing and ultimately helped me to become more financially literate. Similarly, you must always be willing to challenge the people in your circle. Since you know them, you should also know how to challenge them. Encourage them to step outside their comfort zones and watch your circle grow. Remember that a high tide raises all boats!

After challenging Peter, Jesus knew that it was time for the succession. Many times, we only associate the crucifixion with salvation, but it was also Jesus serving as an example. The cross that Jesus carried and ultimately surrendered His life on served as an example to Peter to prepare him for leadership in ministry. Throughout Peter's ministry, many people persecuted him. Every time Peter was persecuted, I believe that he remembered Jesus' endurance and stayed encouraged. You should always know that you are an example for someone else. Your ability to make it through adversity helps others know that they can make it through rough patches.

God fulfills your purpose through those who come after you! For Jesus, His purpose is continuously fulfilled over 2021 years later! You need to take steps to pass the baton in your life. Once you take the right steps, trust in God, and give the baton! The exchange of your legacy will help you win the race that God has marked out for you and those who come after you.

12

Conclusion

Congratulations! You now know how to activate your purpose! *"Activating your purpose"* is more than a phrase; it's a mindset. The first step to being a world changer is to change the way you see the world. The world is waiting for the emergence of leaders, which means the world is waiting for you! "We know that the whole creation has been groaning as in the pains of childbirth right up to the present time" (Romans 8:22). What is creation giving birth to? Leaders. God is calling for a generation to come forth and walk into activated purpose. What if I told you that there is a Promised Land waiting for you? For the Israelites, it was a physical land, but for you, it may look different! Jobs are waiting for you! You are the person that someone is dreaming about right now! Once you believe this, you will wake up each morning with the confidence that God has instilled in you.

Understand it is easier to find purpose than to activate it. Activation requires learning about the purpose that God has given you. It requires you to read the manual. For Christians, our manual is the Bible. The Bible gives us insight and instruction to use our skills and abilities effectively to achieve the purpose that God has for us. The beauty of the Bible is that it is relevant at any point in your life! God has given us the Holy Spirit to serve as His support staff. When trying to figure out your purpose, let the Holy Spirit guide you. The Holy Spirit will help you and even use the Word to point you in the right direction. There are industries that you have not yet even realized that God is waiting for you to enter.

Activating your purpose requires time. There may be times when it feels like God is making you wait for what you believe you are called to do. Understand that God is making you wait because you are in a loading season. Whenever you are downloading something on your phone, you have time to wait for a new application. Why can't we have the same posture for our purpose? See, whenever something is downloading on your phone, the software is being installed. All the software's code, which stores the graphics and functionality, has to be loaded into your phone. During your loading season, God is installing things into you such as patience, stamina, and reliance on Him. This also includes a new mindset!

There was a moment in my own life, where I witnessed God's installation. As an undergraduate student in college, I spent almost half of my time partying. It wasn't until my junior year that I decided that things need to change in my life - mostly for the sake of my grades rather than holiness. However, as I began to take my relationship with God more seriously, I stopped having the urge to hang out and party. Losing the desire to party caused me to look at my social life differently. Since I was not partying, I dedicated that time to God. My friend and I look back and laugh at who we used to be! For you, it might be different! You can still have a good time and live out your purpose! For me, God had to remove some of my previous desires before I could begin to understand my purpose. Your waiting season is essential! Don't think that God has forgotten you; He is only preparing you!

The world is waiting for you!

Lastly, you can't spell activate without "act." Activating your purpose requires you to act. If you think about it, all the disciples were doing something when Jesus called them. Peter was fishing, and Matthew was collecting taxes! The disciples were all diligent in their business whenever Jesus called them. Jesus never criticizes the men for their previous occupations. I believe that these occupations were necessary for their purpose! The same concepts that Peter used to catch fish, he could use to catch the hearts of people. Matthew's persistence with collecting taxes translated to his determination in ministry. For you, don't feel ashamed of your current job or circumstance. You may think that school or working is meaningless, but God has placed you there for a reason. God wants you to be diligent and work towards your purpose. If you are taking action, God will lead you to satisfaction.

If you are serious about God's purpose for your life, everything about you will change! You know the feeling that you get whenever everything seems to be working out! Have you ever driven, and every traffic light is green? What a fantastic feeling! That is the same feeling you have when your purpose is activated! You start living in God's "perfect will" (Romans 12:2)! You begin to realize that everything has purpose. Purpose is not just limited to going to church, singing an occasional Gospel hymn, or praying. Purpose even flows through what you eat, who you talk to, and what you read. Think about it! Even Jesus' naps had purpose! Get ready to live a purpose-filled life. Activate your purpose and change the world!

A couple of months ago, I watched the movie, Soul on Disney Plus. It was a terrific movie about a man in search of his purpose. I won't spoil all the details, but in the film, I had an epiphany. God

To activate your purpose, you must act!

showed me that we don't find purpose, purpose finds us. The more we waste our time searching for our purpose, the more purpose itself becomes our god. Our responsibility is to live each day to its fullest potential. Through living is where we realize our true purpose. That is the essence of Activate Your Purpose! Purpose is not discovered suddenly. It is realized daily. You will face challenging moments in life, and events will occur when you won't understand God's reasoning. If you remain faithful, the good news is that you lived in your purpose the entire time. Once you have realized the purpose is inside of you, it is activated. Now, go and change the world!

Acknowledgements

"Blessed is the one
who does not walk in step with the wicked
or stand in the way that sinners take
or sit in the company of mockers,
but whose delight is in the law of the Lord,
and who meditates on his law day and night.
That person is like a tree planted by streams of water,
which yields its fruit in season
and whose leaf does not wither—
whatever they do prospers" (Psalm 1:1-3)

To everyone who has contributed to the planting, nurturing, and sustenance: thank you!

...stay positive

References

There are endless translations that you can use to find the Scripture references. Below are a couple of links that will help you navigate through the Scriptures found:

"Bible Gateway Passage - New International Version." *Bible Gateway*, www.biblegateway.com/passage/?search.

Staff, BibleStudyTools. *Biblestudytools.com*, BibleStudyTools, www.biblestudytools.com/luke/10-19.html.

"Blue Letter Bible." *Blue Letter Bible*, www.blueletterbible.org/.

"Read the Bible. A Free Bible on Your Phone, Tablet, and Computer." *Read the Bible. A Free Bible on Your Phone, Tablet, and Computer. | The Bible App | Bible.com*, www.bible.com/.

Committed to advancing the Gospel in a fresh way, with the fire of conviction, Collin writes his first book Activate Your Purpose. Growing up in Florence, Collin has spent his entire life in the great state of South Carolina. A 2020 graduate of Clemson University, Collin earned a B.S. in Industrial Engineering with a minor in Business Administration. While at Clemson, Collin led a ministry called, "The 412," which provided a platform for students to grow and learn more about Christ. Collin's focus is to inspire reconnection with Christ in order to build the next generation of leaders.